animaL
TaLK

INTERSPECIES

TELEPATHIC

COMMUNICATION

animal
talk

PENELOPE SMITH

BEYOND
WORDS
Publishing
I N C

Beyond Words Publishing, Inc.
20827 N.W. Cornell Road, Suite 500
Hillsboro, Oregon 97124-9808
503-531-8700

Original edition published in 1982 by Pegasus Publications
Proofreader: Joseph Siegel
Design: Principia Graphica
Composition: William H. Brunson Typography Services
Managing editor: Kathy Matthews

Printed in the United States of America
Distributed to the book trade by Publishers Group West

Library of Congress Cataloging-in-Publication Data
Smith, Penelope.
    Animal talk: interspecies telepathic communication / Penelope Smith.
        p.   cm.
    ISBN 1-58270-001-X (pbk.)
    1. Human—animal communication.   2. Telepathy.   I. Title.
    QL776.S63   1999
    591.59′4—dc21   98-44493
                                                                        CIP

The corporate mission of Beyond Words Publishing, Inc.:
Inspire to Integrity

Contents

INTRODUCTION

a few words

to animal lovers

I'VE LOVED ANIMALS of all kinds as far back as I can remember. I personally can't imagine life on Earth without their myriad forms and styles of life adding to the grace and beauty of the whole environment and enriching our ways to look at life.

Rather than thinking of animals and people as "them" and "us," I see all of Earth's life forms, including plants, rocks, water, air, and all we experience around us, as a symbiotic whole. We are working in concert, unfolding a cycle that we have been developing over the millennia—a continual play to act in, observe, and unravel toward more enjoyment of life and exchange with one another. The harmony is unbalanced when cruelty, misuse, and misunderstanding replace communication, as has often happened in humanity's relationship with the rest of the animal kingdom, to the detriment of all of us in the long run.

Fortunately, throughout all ages, there have been many people who have revered and treated their fellow animals as spiritual brothers and sisters. Communion and communication with other species is not a new idea. This thread can be found woven through the world's religious traditions and as a basic fact of life in tribal communities of many lands. Such outstanding individuals as St. Francis, Albert Schweitzer, Mahatma Gandhi, Jane Goodall, and Francine (Penny) Patterson have exemplified it.

The intention of this book is to continue, restore, and assist this tradition of interspecies connection for those who seek it. Obviously, if you picked up this book you have some affinity for animals or at least curiosity to know more about relating to them. You'll find information here to help you get closer to animals by expanding your ability to communicate with them. May this increase the amount of joy and understanding flowing among all beings in this universe.

THE nature
OF communication
WITH animals

THE WORD *ANIMAL* comes from the Latin, *anima*, which means life principle, breath, air, soul, living being.

Human and nonhuman animals have in common that they are a combination of body and spirit—biological forms animated by spiritual beings or essences. Many people have a hard time accepting the spiritual aspect of animals because they carry established notions that animals are objects or less than human, even robotic creatures with blind instincts and no thoughts or feelings or power of choice. They may use these attitudes to justify or excuse cruel or insensitive treatment of other animals.

For many humans the issue is clouded in that they regard *themselves* as merely bodies or genetic products without awareness of their basic spiritual essence. This can foster disrespect and inhumane actions toward other people as well. It becomes difficult or even impossible for people with this viewpoint to recognize the spiritual nature of other forms of life.

The proof of the spiritual nature of human and nonhuman creatures alike is that when you address them accordingly, with respect and helpfulness, you can improve the condition of the whole being. In my work, a key element is recognizing the individual animal as a spiritual being who is inhabiting or enlivening a particular form. By using this perspective in communication and counseling, upsets and behavior problems are resolved, illnesses and injuries are more readily healed, and the individual becomes more alive, aware, and happy. This would not be possible if I took a completely behaviorist stance, regarding the animal as a complex of automatic or instinctual behaviors with little or no intelligence. Dealing with all aspects of their being—physical, emotional, mental, and spiritual—yields fuller understanding and helpfulness toward all creatures.

As an animal communication specialist, I devote my attention to the subject of living beings, particularly the ones that have four legs and fur or two legs with feathers or other physical features distinct from those of *Homo sapiens*. Thousands of private consultations with animals and their human companions, in person and at a distance, have helped to handle upsets and behavior problems, aid recovery from illness and injury (with the help of needed veterinary care), improve communication with and understanding of animals, and set guidelines for nutritional counseling and body energy balancing. Lectures and workshops focus on helping people to regain their own ability to communicate with animals.

THE INBORN ABILITY
TO COMMUNICATE

People often want to know when I started communicating with animals and how I gained or knew I had the ability to understand what animals are thinking and feeling.

As a child I loved animals, as most children do. I loved touching them and watching them and being close to them. I was able to feel what they felt and understand what their needs were on a very intuitive basis. I could "be" them. Later on, I would talk to them aloud or by thought, and experience answers from them mentally. It was very natural. I knew that they loved me as I did them, and that they could talk to me and think for themselves.

All beings have the inborn ability to communicate with and understand each other. All or most young children can experience mental or telepathic communication with others of any species. It's the main way, along with physical gesture, that they communicate before they learn language.

However, when children learn to speak, they tend to inhibit their ability to communicate directly through thought, since the speaking ability is most validated and encouraged by adults and gets the most attention. So the telepathic ability begins to fade, as any function can when it is not used. In addition, parents and other adults often invalidate a child for any statement like "the dog told me she has a tummy ache." This is made light of as "imagination"—or punished as lying or exaggeration. Obviously, most children learn quickly that the ability to listen to and receive thoughts from animals is not desirable and in fact *does not exist*. They soon suppress the ability, or it disappears, as you cannot retain an ability that you don't believe exists or is impossible.

They may then cease to regard their fellow animals as thinking and feeling beings. Compounding this is a general failure to teach children how to handle animals gently and learn their physical needs. If children mistreat animals, they further separate themselves from wanting to know or understand their spiritual connection with animals. Even when they are very young, children may start making fun of anyone who might mention a mental or spiritual experience beyond what is rigidly accepted as "normal." They emulate what they learn from adults as acceptable beliefs and behavior.

Later in life some fortunate individuals will open up to the fact that mental and spiritual qualities or dimensions beyond the ordinary do indeed exist. They can begin again to experience these qualities by following the successful methods practiced by others throughout the ages in order to recognize and regain innate mental communication abilities.

MY PERSONAL EXPERIENCE

I never lost the ability to communicate with animals. When adults or other children invalidated my experiences of telepathically receiving messages from animals, I decided that it was best to keep these things to myself. Some of my mother's favorite expressions about me were that I had an "active imagination" and that I was "stubborn as a mule." Perhaps both these qualities helped me to retain my telepathic communication capacity!

I did not want to lose the trust and warmth and understanding I had with my animal friends or betray our mutual awareness of their intelligence and shared communication. This was too precious to me to let it be spoiled by others' unawareness. So I continued to curl up with Fritzi, my cat, and know that we understood each other, or enjoy Winkie, my parakeet, sitting on my glasses, delicately preening my eyebrows as I did my homework. I spent hours in the park quietly talking to birds and butterflies to get them to land on my hand. I let them know that I wouldn't hurt them, and I was thrilled when they responded by getting close to me.

When I grew up and left home, for years I had no animal companions of my own, since I was moving around or at college. So I didn't pay much attention to my ability to communicate with animals. It stayed tucked under the surface, much as the knowledge of a foreign language might, until you meet a person who speaks that language.

I studied the social sciences, hoping to learn more about understanding and helping to improve the condition of human beings, which has always been a basic purpose of mine. In 1971, I was again in the position to have animal companions. I had also acquired much desired knowledge and practical methodology to help the human mind and spirit by training and working as a counselor.

My ability to communicate with animals took on a new dimension. Besides being able to talk and listen to animals, I had acquired tools to help them. I found that the same techniques for helping people release past traumas, relieve emotional upsets, and handle problems and mental blocks helped animals also.

My first animal client was Peaches, a small, black and white female cat who was left with me when her person could no longer care for her. She was definitely a "scaredy-cat." She would run and hide from people and was afraid of other cats in the neighborhood.

A few weeks after her arrival, she came in with a bloody bite on her back, where another cat had attacked her. I cleaned and put ointment on it, expecting it to heal with no problem. Peaches, however, had other ideas. As soon as it would scab over, she'd scratch it open. Bandages and soothing preparations were to no avail, as she was determined to get at that wound. The bloody area was no longer the original half-inch bite but now extended two or three inches, and the hair around the area was falling out. She looked gruesome, and my roommates were beginning to complain about doing something with that cat.

So, I sat with Peaches across from me on a chair and decided to counsel her as I would a human being in trouble. I asked her specific questions about the physical trauma and her feelings, and she answered me telepathically. She relayed to me many mental pictures of other cats scaring and attacking her. By facing up to these frightening incidents, she released a lot of emotional charge and felt much better.

We continued with our counseling session, and she discovered that keeping the wound there and making it worse was actually a solution to the problem she felt of being afraid of people and other animals. She had figured that if she made her body very ugly, people and cats would stay away from her. It was working, though making her life miserable in the process. When she uncovered and fully brought to her awareness this subconscious decision, she visibly became very peaceful and purred happily.

The remarkable results of this session were that, by the next day, her wound had scabbed over, and in about one week the hair had grown back so you couldn't tell she had ever been hurt. Even more amazing was that Peaches was a changed individual. No longer did she run away when anyone entered the room, but instead she curled up on their lap and purred! The cats in the neighborhood no longer singled her out for attacks. She didn't attract that anymore.

I learned that not only do animals think, feel, understand, and communicate, but also that the principles and methods used for alleviating human mental blocks and increasing harmony in living could bring incredible improvements to other species as well.

I did not immediately hang out a shingle as an "animal communication specialist." My work as human counselor and my own spiritual expansion continued. In 1976, I pursued an area of interest that I had long abandoned, the field of dance, and began to perform and teach dance as my main occupation. However, after doing successful animal consultations among friends, the word of this skill spread, and my work with animals became more than a sideline. In 1977, I officially became a professional animal communication specialist by charging fees for my services.

Dance was still my main focus until 1979, when I traveled and trained other instructors in my movement techniques and then wrote several books on dance and body movement.

As my emphasis shifted more to working with animals, and the results of my work became known, I was interviewed for hundreds of radio stations nationwide, appeared on TV programs and in newspapers, and wrote articles for various publications. Since that time I have consulted with thousands of animals and their people and given many lectures and workshops on communication with animals.

HOW ANIMALS COMMUNICATE

Popular psychology promotes some common but uninsightful notions about animal communication and intelligence: Because most animals have less complexly structured brains than humans, they therefore have less intelligence and no real emotions or reasoning power, and communicate only in rudimentary ways, such as grunts, barks, whistles, and other body signals. These notions are changing as scientists continue to discover the complexity of meanings present in the sounds and gestures of creatures from bees to birds to apes. Many are beginning to observe, with less human-centered bias, the intricate and demonstrably intelligent behavioral responses of animals. There is, of course, much more to learn from the animals themselves by direct telepathic communication, the universal language. That will come with increased observation skills and awareness.

Intelligence, according to *Webster's Dictionary*, is *the ability to learn or understand from experience, or the ability to respond quickly and successfully to a new situation.* Using this definition, I'm sure you can think of many examples of animal intelligence, such as incidents of cats or dogs who have traveled thousands of miles to find the people who left them behind when they moved, or the resourcefulness of rats, raccoons, coyotes, and other wild animals in surviving among human habitation when people have taken over their natural environment.

It does not make sense to measure animal intelligence by the often-assumed standard of how closely an animal can resemble human behavior. Animals have different genetic makeups and physical capacities. Their responses vary according to their type of body, environment, and experience.

One of the main physical differences that enables humans to accomplish many tasks and express their intelligence in ways that other members of the animal kingdom cannot, is extremely flexible and highly developed hands and nervous systems that allow a wide range of manipulative ability. The fact that animals cannot write letters or play the guitar does not mean they are not intelligent.

Are humans considered less intelligent because they cannot fly like birds or run as fast as cheetahs? These are the result of body differences, not mental capacity. The same spiritual being inhabiting a human body and using it to design and build houses would create a nest of leaves and twigs if dwelling in a bird's body. She or he would still be the same intelligent being, but would be using a different body according to its physical capacities.

While the human body may enable more complex or varied ways to express intelligence, the complexity and diversity of other creatures' expression are also amazing. Differences among species are definitely present. This does not necessarily imply superiority or inferiority. We are all different, which makes life so interesting.

Beings develop and use their bodies according to their genetic capacities and the situations with which they are faced.

Some do it more successfully or intelligently than others. Most domesticated animals have mastered the art of living with humans so well that they fit among, influence, and, in some cases, control human activity.

Individual animals differ from each other in levels of intelligence, sensitivity, and ability to communicate well, as do individual human beings. Some are more aware and more interested than others, and it's easier to engage in communication with them.

Some are really into being a dog, cat, or horse, for example, and follow the body's impulses and genetic heritage closely. Others set their own style as individuals in addition to how their bodies naturally tend. They are willing and able to control their body impulses and adapt to the situation in which they live, such as being more like the people around them.

Most animals are willing to come into a closer relationship if they are understood as they are and approached from their level of awareness. In some cases they are more perceptive or aware than the humans who attempt to understand them.

Animals obviously communicate through physical action, but they also communicate through direct thought, feeling, intention, and mental pictures, both among each other and with humans. People receive the telepathic messages to the degree they are listening, can tune in, or are perceptive to them.

While I often use physical contact to help establish rapport and to assist animals in distress, I communicate mainly telepathically or by direct thought and feeling transmission, silently or accompanied by spoken words. Though many animals understand words, owing to familiarity with human language, they innately get your intentions, emotions, images, or thoughts behind the words, even if the words themselves aren't totally understood. Since animals are not forced into the idea that words or symbols are the only or ultimate way to communicate, they do not lose their innate telepathic sensitivity and ability as most humans do.

When they communicate their thoughts and feelings to me, I get what they mean and usually translate their communication into words instantly, as that's what I and other humans are accustomed to. When they're describing a scene or something that happened to them, I see the scene from their viewpoint, mentally perceiving and feeling the sights, sounds, emotions, and other senses as they experienced them. If you've ever had the experience of knowing what some other person is thinking, perhaps even saying aloud the same thought simultaneously, or really getting another person's mental pictures or feelings, you'll get the idea of how I communicate with animals regularly, and how you can, too.

Animals do understand what you say or think to them, that is, if you have their attention and they want to listen (just like anyone else). One of the ways some animals get away with not having to do what you want is by pretending that they don't understand. Often humans perpetuate this by considering that their dog (cat, bird, horse, tortoise) is dumb, doesn't understand anything, or can't really feel like they do. Some people even name their animal companions "Dodo" or "Dimwit" or some other insult to their intelligence. Many animals, like many children, play the game you expect from them, and act dumb. Then they don't have to be responsive to your demands.

The interesting thing is that the more you respect animals' intelligence, talk to them conversationally, include them in your life, and regard them as friends, the more intelligent and warm responses you'll usually get. Beings of all kinds tend to flower when they are showered with warmth and understanding from others.

I observed an interesting example of this at a boarding school I visited. There I met an Irish wolfhound, whom I immediately perceived as very knowing and perceptive about what was going on in the area. However, the consensus from the people around was that he was very stupid and couldn't do much of anything right. This was evidenced, I was told, by his slow response to doing anything anyone told him and the way he stupidly ambled into the school and lounged on the rugs and cozy furniture, even though any smart dog would know from the number of people who reprimanded him that such actions weren't okay.

When they told me in his presence that he was really stupid, he flashed me with the thoughts, "Don't let them know what I'm doing—it's my game." (Note that these words are my translation of the dog's concept. Sometimes animals will transmit verbal phrases that they have picked up, but most of the time the words are an approximation in human language of the thought and feeling sent.) I laughed, as this dog was very much in control of what people thought of him and the life he was leading, doing only what he wanted to, watching everyone around him, observing and learning from their activities.

Despite his warning, I felt it my duty to clear up this invalidation of his mental capacity, and so I explained that he was very intelligent and knew exactly what was going on and what people told him. He was a little angry with me for telling on him, since people might expect more of him, but I couldn't bear the lie of his dumbness to be perpetuated. I communicated further with him later when he was willing to talk, and he decided it might be a nice thing to be more responsive to people and make their lives more cheerful.

I still chuckle when I think of how he had everyone fooled—and that's not intelligent?

Of course, nonhuman animals, like humans, can misunderstand a communication and not know what you are trying to say to them, especially if you are unclear on what you want from them. They can be distracted by what is occurring, especially by things attractive to their biological needs, like food smells or other animals, and not pay attention to your communication. You have to get their attention and communicate within the realm of their experience.

Asking cats to play a piano concerto will probably not make sense to them, so they will not respond well to your request. You also need to like and respect animals and allow them to be the way they are—living beings who have their own desires and choices and are influenced by their particular genetic inheritance in varying degrees, as we all are.

You can learn from your own animal friends, who usually ask from you only those things that are within your ability to provide. They like and accept you as you are. They generally love your attempts to communicate with them and really appreciate your affection and understanding.

People often ask what kind of animal is the most intelligent. It's hard to make a general statement, as different bodies have different functions. What would be considered intelligent in operating one kind of body would not be intelligent in handling another.

More complex bodies with more highly developed brains seem to have more choices programmed into their "computers," although I have experienced "advanced" communications from "lower" forms, such as insects—similar to J. Allen Boone's experience with a fly he called Freddy, in his book (which I highly recommend), *Kinship with All Life*.

What animals do with the limitations of their type of body program varies among individuals of any species. In general, the larger animals and those who most easily demonstrate a willingness to communicate with humans and learn their ways are often considered more flexible, responsive, or intelligent—e.g., whales, dolphins, elephants, apes, horses, dogs, cats, and other domesticated animals. However, one can also find very intelligent or wise beings in less complex forms on the body scale. For example, people have been amazed at the brightness and intensity of communication from members of my animal family, such as a box turtle, Marla, an anole lizard, Ginko, or a guinea pig, Cinnamon.

No two whales, dogs, or cats are exactly alike in intelligence, communication level, or emotional response. Also, one's own ability to perceive animals as fellow beings and to relate with them in an intelligent way might yield very different assessments. Some animals that were considered slow or stupid by some people, I have found to be wonderful to talk to, with many fine qualities that their people missed.

The great thing is that we can all learn from each other. Individual people can demonstrate their own intelligence by willingness to observe, learn about, and understand animals better. People, of course, will vary in their willingness.

restoring the

telepathic

connection

Wнат is interspecies telepathic communication? *Tele-* refers to distance, and *-pathy* refers to feeling. So, telepathic communication involves the ability to feel another across a distance. It is not just a test of mental agility or ability reserved for a small percentage of the population that is especially gifted or sensitive. It is an inborn capacity of all species, including humans. More than anything else, telepathy is a connection, a direct link to the soul of all beings. It's a mindful, yet "mind-less" understanding—a knowing of what the other is thinking, feeling, and experiencing, so directly that one being almost becomes the other.

Such contact is based on the recognition that all beings are intelligent and that they can understand, interrelate, and communicate. It's the experience of receiving direct thought transmission, images, feelings, and concepts from individuals of other species, repeatedly confirmed by often drastic changes in behavior and enhancement of cooperation, peacefulness, and closeness. It is not dependent on distance. Telepathic communication can occur between beings across many miles, through walls and other barriers. It is dependent on making the connection, tuning in and knowing with whom you're communicating—similar to getting the right phone number or the proper radio station.

Where human and nonhuman beings walk together in mutual understanding, the nobility and individuality of both are called forth. Harmony, dignity, and mutual respect usually replace fear and aggression. Even skeptical people can see the difference after a true telepathic exchange wherein rapport has occurred between humans and other species.

It is vastly different from the desperately needy state of many humans with their "pets." I prefer not to use the word pet because of its connotations of dependence, condescension, disposability, and possession. Instead, I use terms that seem to me more dignified: *animal companion* or *animal friend*.

An example of the imbalance of many human–pet relationships was brought graphically to my attention when I appeared on a television talk show in New York City. The hostess of the show had two Lhasa apso dogs who were scheduled to be interviewed by me on the show. I met them beforehand, and the hostess asked me how they seemed. She considered them her babies and desperately wanted them to be okay. Her voice and eyes were filled with anxiety as she said she hoped they would not say anything bad about her on television. She depended on her dogs for love, for life, and there couldn't be anything "wrong" with them. I felt the dogs trying to fill her need, and being totally dependent on her. She was seeking to get the wholeness from them that she lacked in her hectic, disconnected life. The interview was cut for lack of time before the dogs had a chance to communicate and "tell all."

Animals can get caught up in their humans' imbalances, because of their dependency and also their deep desire to serve and help their human friends. Sickness can result when the animal attempts to heal or take away human misery or to mirror it. Sometimes they just feel its vibration because of their proximity and devotion. "Pets" are often prevented from living a life close to their own nature. They aren't able to release imbalances easily if they do not have access to fresh air, exercise, a whole-food diet, natural exploration, and independence. Divorced from nature, they may suffer from the same "dis-eases" that their people endure.

How different the relationship is when our domestic animal friends are viewed as fellow spiritual beings of different forms and allowed to live their own lives and express their own dignity, while still enjoying a mutual companionship with us and each other. Many people who meet members of my animal family notice how relaxed, happy, and independent they are. They come and go and create relationships of their choosing with their own species, humans, and other species. They are regarded as wise, intelligent individuals, who are cats, dogs, rats, chickens, horses, and more—the "anima" in animal—the spirit, soul, life essence. They act as whole, individual characters with their own dignity, quirks, rights, needs, expressions, and understanding of the balance of our family or community. We adapt and change according to our mutual growth and understanding. We listen to each other and work out agreements in accord with our needs and environment. It's a fun place to be for all of us.

As people divorce themselves from nature, from the spiritual essence that flows through all of life, and place great emphasis on pursuing material goods for status, their relationship with their fellow creatures of different forms often assumes the shallow character of owner and possession. Without the spiritual connection, even when they profess love for their "pets," they may neurotically try to get from them all that they have given up in their own artificial quest. The animals mirror their misery.

When people give their animal friends more credit, the animals appreciate it deeply, perk up, and cooperate more. As people begin to restore their ability to listen fully to their animal companions, problems get solved without forceful and strange solutions, such as sticking animals' faces in their own excrement or beating them.

Practicing the way of connection and communion takes some effort. It represents a shift from frenetic, materialistically oriented lifestyles to calmer, more observant, caring ways of life—a profound leap in consciousness for many. The benefits are immense for all of us.

OPENING TO TELEPATHY

As a very young child, I sensed what people were thinking and feeling, whom they were deep inside, and why they were the way they were. I observed how people closed themselves off to seeing what was right before their eyes. I knew that animals were intelligent beings who could understand each other and me, and that we were alike, except for our physical appearance.

My mother insisted that I had a very active imagination—and I did. I could "see" the thoughts, intentions, and images behind words and physical forms. I felt a whole world of spirit around me—angels, guides, saints, fairies, and other disembodied spirits. I wondered why others couldn't see or didn't want to see. I was spirit, and I knew spirit was everywhere, in everything, and surrounding everything.

Throughout my childhood, our family had a parade of animal companions: goldfish, turtles, parakeets, cats, and dogs. My closest animal friends were Winky, a blue parakeet, and Fritzi, a male calico cat.

Winky was my companion when I was about eleven years old. Through homework assignments, he perched on my glasses and preened my eyelashes and eyebrows. We gave each other hours of loving companionship, and I delighted in caring for him. One day Winky bit me hard on the nose, and I reacted in shock and pain by hitting him. I immediately regretted my action, as the blow slammed him against the wall. I tried to make it up to him, but Winky never forgot, and our relationship was irretrievably altered.

Soon afterwards he began to have seizures, flailing around his cage and spitting blood. I took him to the pet store, where they gave him medication and charged me an enormous amount of my hard-earned allowance, but it didn't help. The seizures got worse, although he acted normal when out of the cage. Winky bit me again, and we fell further apart.

I didn't have the counseling skills then to handle the emotional cause of his illness, but I knew the seizures were because of our upset. My older brother agreed to take Winky to his home and take care of him. Winky never had a seizure again while he lived for many years with my brother. I always remembered our happy times together, and along the way the wound between us healed.

Our cat Fritzi liked all of us in our family of eight people, especially my father. My mother complained that we kids couldn't really love him as we said we did if we didn't clean his litter box, a job she hated. After I gladly took over the task and parked the litter box in my bedroom, Fritzi and I became very close. I would curl up in bed in the same scimitar shape that Fritzi assumed, and we'd sleep together like two crescent moons. We took refuge in our bedroom to avoid the frequent parental conflicts accentuated by alcohol. Fritzi and I understood each other deeply.

When I left home to enter the convent and start my college education in September 1964, Fritzi did not fare well. Beginning the first day after I left, he had several bouts of intestinal and kidney disease and he died months later.

Years later I took a college psychology course, which presented animal (including human) behavior from a mechanistic viewpoint, focusing on experiments with rats in mazes and dogs salivating. I decided to adopt the materialistic viewpoint that was expressed in this type of course and in the college students around me. Not only would I take the "psyche" (spirit) out of psychology as the college courses did, but I would take the spirit out of life and assume, as others did, that all of us, of whatever species, were nothing but material forms, created by accidental particle collision and ending in dissolution of molecules.

With spirit denied, I immediately felt the despair, the drabness of existence that many people in our culture experience. I felt there was no point to anything, no purpose, no color, no feeling, just randomly organized motion. I realized why many college students rushed to bars and filled themselves up with "spirit" from bottles. They were empty, and life was bitter and meaningless. They needed some escape, some way to release and connect with the larger picture, even if it meant oblivion. I understood why my parents, who denied themselves as spiritual beings and felt such fear and hate, were alcoholics. I understood why my mother was often so disturbed by my presence, especially my singing and dancing, which affirmed the true self that she tried to deny. I also understood what leads some people to the desperate pursuit of material success or to suicide: a perspective that made life look so bleak and unhappy.

I could sustain the grim, behaviorist, materialistic attitude for only a few days. Then I returned to a revitalized understanding of myself and all of life around me, infused with spirit, love for life, and hope for harmony. This is the reason I couldn't renounce telepathic communication with animals and other spirits. It was too true, too real, too much fun—and I couldn't betray my animal friends by denying their inner life, thoughts, and feelings, which they so graciously and happily shared with me. So I didn't, and the ability never died.

For those of you who have long buried the natural ability to connect with others telepathically and have accepted the cultural conditioning that this is not possible or is hocus-pocus, unscientific nonsense, it may take time and practice to renew the freshness of outlook that is conducive to two-way communication with other species. Learn from little children to open your heart and mind; learn from the love of animals and all of life around you.

This is a spiritual path that will require change, a turning over of many socially conditioned habits and patterns. More people every day are reconnecting with their ability to understand other species, but you may not be greeted in your home or at work with jubilation over your newfound ability. In fact, others may find it threatening that you can receive other animals' thoughts, because it may mean you will be more receptive to human thinking, feeling, and intentions and less under their control.

My feeling is that we may grow spiritually—not up or down, to different levels in unending hierarchies, but by extending outwards in a circular, encompassing way, to include and understand more of life. Instead of looking down at others "below" us condescendingly as we evolve, we enfold life in all its forms with more compassion, understanding, grace, and wisdom.

PREPARING FOR COMMUNICATION

To regain the telepathic connection requires that you dismantle learned, culturally conditioned obstacles to your native ability to connect, communicate, and understand animals. Allow yourself to open the door and move along the path to your own potential for reconnection. In my workshops, we apply principles that help open that door. We will review some of them here.

To be receptive and listen to anyone, of whatever species, requires a quiet attention, a calmness, that many humans in our industrialized, commercialized cities and revved-up lifestyles have displaced long ago. We live in an age of speed, where people are constantly being fed one jarring stimulus after another. Traffic, crowding, crimes, television, and advertisements all jam our senses, our receptive equipment, so that we shut down our sensitivity to the world around us just to survive.

We learn not to pay attention. Many advertisers think that we have to be slammed with information, assertively and repetitively, because we're so overwhelmed with incoming information. So we build psychic walls. We cease to see, hear, feel, smell, much of what's around us. We listen to no one, often including our own inner selves and feelings. Whew! What a legacy to overcome.

Animals are naturally able to tune in telepathically with each other and with any other species. They can receive thoughts, mental images, emotions, intentions, and messages when they are willing and attentive. What about humans? How can we restore our birthright, lost through social conditioning—the ability to telepathically communicate, to send and receive communication outside the confines of human language?

As babies and small children, we were open to the world, eager and curious—open to the sights, sounds, feelings, and thoughts of all the beings around us. Children often talk to their animal companions and know that the animals understand and can communicate back to them.

What happens to adults that they stand there dully and don't see and hear the communication of animals?

Humans are the most socially conditioned of all species. In our culture at this time, telepathic communication is not generally accepted openly. We learn our verbal language, and that's supposed to suffice. We're not supposed to know anything other than what we receive through the confirmation of words. This is odd, for if you don't understand the thoughts and feelings behind the words—the true meaning of what people communicate—then you don't really understand the words anyway. In true communication among people, dictionary definitions are not enough.

Human language, as removed as it may be from direct thought transmission, requires reception of thoughts and feelings to be complete. Whether we realize it or not, we all, to some degree, telepathically communicate with each other. We lose or cover up our telepathic communication skills to the degree we consider it impossible or undesirable.

Since we are also socialized to believe that animals cannot think—at least, not as we do—and are below us, we lose touch with them on this very direct and deep level. Other species, which are not socialized out of the ability, never lose telepathic connection with each other and with us. We close off telepathic reception, and we are the losers, the lesser skilled. We limit ourselves, and because we don't understand the animals, we call their behavior and intelligence limited—a turned-around state of affairs, to be sure.

Modern life in general motivates us to close off our sensitivity and deny the subtle realities, the communication of thought and feeling all around us. We end up with a manic impulse to keep up with all the expectations of the culture around us, so that we rarely or never have a quiet mind, a peaceful outlook, and a calm receptivity.

So, the first step in learning to communicate with anyone is to calm the buzzing of thoughts in our own heads. We need to slow down, let the thoughts run through their course, and become calmly aware of the environment and the beings in it. You can't receive another's thoughts if your own mind is too busy. If you are constantly analyzing and projecting your own thoughts and images, you won't see what's there, you won't be able to receive and learn from others, and you won't understand another's viewpoint. You need to shift the hectic mode of approaching the world and come to quietude. Whatever helps you to relax and be aware—exercise, meditation, music—can start you on the road to receptivity.

When you do slow down and tune in, you may find yourself much more aware of the nature of life around you—the behavior, habits, feelings, energies, and the spirit or essence of life forms. You may find, as you continue to spend time in a quiet, receptive mode with other species, that they initiate communications with you. Generally, when a person is listening, others enjoy "talking" with them.

EXTENDED SENSE CHANNELS

The animals are practiced in catching your thoughts, images, or intentions. How will you get what *they* are "saying"? Telepathic communication comes across in different ways. You may detect emotions, images, impressions, thoughts, intentions, messages, feelings, or energies in different forms, which unfold in ways that you can learn to interpret or understand.

Each person has sense channels by which she or he most readily accesses interspecies communication. Many people are able to receive feelings or emotions from others and get a sense of what's going on with them. Some people are more visually oriented and receive mental images or impressions of colors, scenes, objects, or events. Others "hear" messages, sounds, voices, words—that is, they receive auditory impressions. Some pick up the animal's thoughts or concepts, which they can translate or express in words. Some get smells, tastes, tactile sensations, and physical feelings that they experience in the animal they are communicating with or they sense in their own bodies while in contact with the animal. Some people just "know" what the animal is feeling or thinking; they get a direct perception or knowing, which they can translate into words, images, and feelings.

All modes of reception are possible, even experienced during the same communication, as a complete package of sensory impressions. As you continue to practice receiving telepathically, you may find that more sense channels are open to you, and you may receive communications in any or all of these forms. The more complete your reception of the communication from another animal, the more easily you are able to grasp its whole significance or the depth of its meaning.

Telepathy does not always translate in the same mode from sender to receiver. If an animal is sending visual images, and you are more receptive to emotions or feelings, you may pick up the message in an emotive way and understand that. Or the animal may be sending a thought message, but you receive and understand it as impressions and sensations. Just as a radio is designed to receive signals and translate them into sound, you may perform a similar translation. It doesn't matter as long as there is understanding of what was communicated.

How animals transmit is not necessarily a function of their species' physical predispositions, such as greater acuity in sight or smell. Telepathy is a mental or spiritual ability, not limited to bodily organs.

When people begin learning to communicate telepathically, they often receive impressions that they don't know how to interpret or that seem fragmented. Learn to take what you get, and let it gel or unfold. You can also ask the animal more about what their communication means, or for more details. As you gain experience with a multitude of beings, you become more able to make sense of what you get, and it fits better into the total picture.

Every communication and every individual is unique and should not be lumped together or passed off as "just like the last one," if you wish to fully understand that moment and that individual's unique expression. You will see patterns stemming from species or breed similarities and unity among spirit of all forms, but be careful about categorizing or stereotyping anyone's communication. Be ever open to surprises, or you may deny yourself understanding by ceasing to truly listen.

RECEPTIVITY VS. PROJECTION

Now for the big question asked by most people who are learning to communicate with animals: *How do you know you're getting communication from the animal and not just a projection of your own thoughts or feelings?*

First, you need to be quiet, not thinking or expecting anything in particular, but being calm and receptive with an open heart and mind. Then, when another wishes to communicate something to you, or you ask them about something, you will receive their thoughts and feelings, not your own. Your own thoughts do not intrude, but stay in their place in the background.

You need to practice maintaining a quiet receptiveness. In our culture, we have been trained to use predominantly left-brain skills—to analyze, categorize, judge, and project, to keep up with the pace and be sharp-witted. For many people, these habits are not balanced easily with right-brain openness to the whole picture.

This initial and essential approach is the opposite of jumping in and figuring things out sequentially. It's backing up, letting yourself breathe deeply and slowly, experiencing the rhythms of other beings and the universe around you. Then, their thoughts and feelings come in like waves on the beach, with no resistance or thrusting back from you—just a quiet acceptance and understanding and willingness to learn more. If you try too hard to receive communication or expect it to arrive in a certain form, you can miss its simplicity and immediacy. Allow it to be as easy as having a conversation with a dear friend.

Sigh like the wind—open your arms, your chest, your heart—and all creatures will hum to you. They will answer your questions about themselves and the nature of the universe. You'll see for yourself that all of us have our deepest natures, the universal truths, and the essence of spirit in common. We can learn from the smallest creatures, whether microbe or insect, to the largest whale or elephant.

RELEASING
EMOTIONAL BLOCKS

People often find that emotional upsets with, or losses of, animals in their past cause them to block telepathic communication with animals now. They are afraid to get close again and worry that what the animal says will bring back pain that they have buried or not fully faced. Opening up to others on a deep and direct level is a process of growth, requiring the release of accumulated emotional baggage that is in the way.

Maureen Hall tells about her experience at my home in 1990:

Being at the advanced workshop last September made me realize that I needed to really do this kind of work, not just use it occasionally as I have been doing all of my life.

I felt at ease and very natural communicating with your animals. However, I did encounter one very emotional exercise while there. So much so, I couldn't discuss it that day. When we went down to the woods, the place you called the Alder Cathedral, you asked us to ask for an animal guide. I thought it would be nice to be accompanied by the spirit of my little red fox that was with me for sixteen years. However, he did not show up. So I called upon my raccoon of several years ago. She showed up for only a moment, then disappeared. In her place came a dog I had when I was nine years old. This was a dog with which I was very close. A spiritual counselor once told me (although I had never mentioned any past dog to her) that when I was nine I had a dog that saved my life just by being there during a time when I was very ill, and that I had lost this dog in a very traumatic way, and because of that I had held back my psychic abilities. I was afraid to get that close again.

Anyhow, the dog walked with me to the top of the hill, but would not go down the other side with me. I called him, but he said, "No, it is time for me to return. I just wanted you to know that everything is all right and that it is time for you to accept the past and go on with your work."

So now, whenever I feel a hesitation, I think of his words and go ahead. In fact, I have been all but grabbing people off the street and teaching them! And I am totally amazed at how fast everyone picks it up. I feel so good about it, as it is certainly something the world needs to know.

My lectures attract animal lovers from many stations in life. When I speak to a group, I tailor my subject matter and examples to the thoughts I get from the people in the audience about what they wish to know and would benefit from hearing. I remember a lecture with about sixty people in the Los Angeles area, where a man stood in the back with his arms folded across his chest. His facial muscles were tight; his expression was resistant. As I spoke, I particularly addressed him with an example of people being very close to their animal friends and telepathic with them in childhood but how they lose that with adult invalidation or cultural disapproval. After the lecture, when I was answering people's questions, I didn't see him again.

The next day I did a number of consultations for people in the area, and I was called to the home of a woman with several dogs. She thanked me for a wonderful lecture and said that a miraculous change had come over her husband because of it.

After they returned home from the lecture, he began to talk about the animals he had loved as a child. He cried intermittently for hours as he released his suppressed feelings. She explained that he was a policeman in a crime-ridden area, and he had to shut off his feelings to handle his tough work. In their seventeen years of marriage, she had never seen him cry, and she felt their whole relationship had deepened because of this change in him.

He was the man in the back of the lecture hall with his arms folded.

Fear of animals and what they might do to you can inhibit opening to their communication. If you are conditioned into thinking that snakes or spiders are out to get you, it is hard to relax in their company. I experienced the deep emotional effects of cultural conditioning when I first met a scorpion. We had just moved to the woods, and I was arranging a pile of logs near the woodstove in the basement guest room, when I saw what I thought was a big golden-brown beetle. I peered down for a closer look and realized by the upraised tail that it was a scorpion. All I knew about scorpions was from stories and movies about their deadly poison. Immediately my body flushed with fear, and my knees quivered like jelly.

The scorpion merely sat there on the floor. I realized how I was reacting and calmed myself enough to get in touch and communicate with him. I wondered why the scorpion was there, and he explained that he sought damp, dark places. The woodpile in the basement was perfect. He meant me no harm, and he warily wondered what I was going to do. I found a cup and told him I was going to scoop him up and take him outside, where he could live in the woods. He offered no resistance and went on his way as I lowered him to the leaves underneath a bush.

As I read about scorpions in a reference book, the residues of my shock and fear subsided. The scorpions in our area have a sting that is similar to that of a bee and is not deadly like the concentrated venom of some desert scorpions. With this knowledge and my communication experience with the scorpion, I never reacted fearfully when I again encountered scorpions, knowing that their nature was gentle and that they had no intention to harm me.

True communication brings understanding and replaces fear. Except for a few animals who are potential predators of humans, or ones acting in defense of self, their offspring, or their territory, most encounters with animals who are approached quietly and respectfully are rewarded with communication and understanding.

Some people find that the animals they dislike, have an allergic reaction to, or fear seem to be drawn to them. What you fear or resist may "dog" (or "cat" or "spider") you until you accept it. When you immediately withdraw from something, you create a vacuum that seems to attract what you are trying to avoid.

Animals are very good at picking up emotions, especially strong ones like fear. Some animals will respond by wanting to comfort you and help you through your fear. Others perceive there might be some danger or something you're hiding behind the fearfulness and want to guard their people or territory from you and may even attack. Others just accept you the way you are, and attempt to give you warmth and love.

If you are simply honest with them about your feelings or thoughts, most animals respond by being honest and helpful with you. When I first started communicating with horses, I had no experience with them, other than getting my picture taken as a child on a Shetland pony. Through my openly admitting to them my ignorance about how I should act around their large bodies and about what their lives were like, they responded positively to me, leading to my learning a tremendous amount from them. Animals know and respond to the intention behind your words or appearance, so you might as well be honest and direct with them in the first place; then you'll get through your misgivings and more readily establish rapport with them.

Many people have found that changing their attitudes toward animals is the first step to being receptive to what animals have to communicate. People have reported that once they changed their ideas about animals as things or underlings or babies or soulless or unevolved or inferior—regarding them instead as brothers and sisters, with respect and appreciation—they not only related more positively to the animals, but also the animals responded more positively to them. Negative attitudes toward animals can be so pervasive and unexamined. People often don't realize until after they hear about animal intelligence and awareness how neglectful, disrespectful, and even abusive they have been. How wonderful it is to establish or revitalize the deep communion that is possible with our fellow travelers of other species!

THE ROLE OF DIET

Over the years of counseling people and training others in telepathic communication with animals, I have noticed that poor diet, especially overconsumption of sugar, can block telepathic reception. Very sincere people who love animals may find that they have great difficulty in getting animals' messages when they themselves are improperly nourished or addicted to sugary foods. They run into exhaustion, mental blankness, or even black out when they try to deeply tune into an animal who is communicating to them. They may also feel uncomfortable about being alone or doing quiet meditation, and must keep busy.

Some people think that they can concentrate on spiritual practices and advance spiritually while ignoring their bodies. They may consider the body and its impulses to be a lower or less important aspect of self, or they just don't like their bodies and want to deny their physical nature. These attitudes may result in a painful existence. Part of our spiritual task is to care for our vehicle, or temple of the spirit, and enjoy being incarnate on the Earth. Animal lovers may find it helpful to relate to their bodies as their nearest and dearest animal companions that need loving care, good food, and physical exercise to be happy and give good energy in return.

Many people may have to work with emotional or mental conditions that are affecting their dietary decisions before they can

permanently change. However, most mental and spiritual counseling does not have deep or lasting effects without first paying
attention to the basic physical needs of the body for good diet and
exercise. It takes knowledge of the body and personal discipline to
improve on all levels.

A wholesome diet geared for your particular body type and
individual needs helps you stay in balance and be consistent and
clear in your telepathic work with animals. People can get irritable, moody, erratic in behavior, and spaced out if they ignore their
bodies and try to just focus on the spiritual realm. Perhaps you
have met people who are like that.

Regular consumption of a large amount of sugar in your diet is
a proven way to weaken your body's energy flows and immune system. While temporarily pumping blood sugar levels up and
increasing energy, eating a lot of sugary foods exhausts the vital
organs that are responsible for keeping blood sugar balanced.
Energy gets blocked, drained, or dispersed in the body, which
invites dis-ease. The energy current through the chakras (energy
vortices) from the base of the spine to the top of the head is short-
circuited, so that clear perception and reception may be impaired.

Excessive consumption of caffeine in coffee or colas can
restrict or narrow perception, making it difficult to get the whole
picture of what animals are communicating, and who they are.
Other nonnutritive substances have other effects that can be
detrimental to full, grounded connection and communication.

Communicating fully with other beings requires the ground-
ing of energy through the whole body into the Earth and free-
flowing energy through all the nerve channels, the brain, and

sense organs. When you are communicating on this plane, communication is not divorced from the body. Regular ingestion of devitalized food such as sugar, over-processed products, or any food that creates an allergic or clogging reaction strains your nervous system and can create negative physical, emotional, and spiritual conditions.

Consistent success in the field of interspecies telepathic communication, or in any field that requires sensitivity to others' emotional, mental, and spiritual states, requires that one take good care of oneself on all levels. Finding the right balance of whole, fresh foods that work for your body, along with exercise and contact with all the elements of nature, is vital to learning and doing this type of work well.

Integrating—or feeling as one being, whole in body, mind, and spirit—is our task. Ask the animals, especially wild ones, whose diet and exercise patterns have not been altered from their natural form by humans. They will teach you how to enjoy the body fully while deeply experiencing your spiritual nature. Join them in their vitality, balance, and communication with Mother Earth.

LOVE AND TELEPATHY

While visiting with Toby, a white and sky-blue parakeet companion of Nancy Sondel, I playfully asked him, as he sat on my finger, "Toby, what are the Secrets of the Universe?"

He answered, "Love—that's all there is. It's that simple. Love."

Prodding him further, I asked, "Are there any other Secrets?"

"Just love. I'll show you." Toby then surrounded me with a warm, white light, and I experienced his answer permeating all around and through us.

What does love have to do with telepathic communication with other species?

In college I devised a psychology experiment on mental telepathy showing that spontaneous telepathy involves people who are close and that their emotional connection provides a channel for telepathic communication. The emotional bond between people and their animal companions can create a deep telepathic knowing. However, many people find, when they are working to regain their telepathic ability, that they cannot easily receive telepathic communication from members of their own animal family. They often receive much more easily from other people's animal friends. Why is this?

We get back to that word *love* again. Practicing love as acceptance, respect, reverence, good will, caring, brother/sisterhood, and even devotion is an important part of making a connection that is sufficient to promote the deep sensing and reception consistent with telepathic contact. Toby relayed love to me as a full sensing of connection, recognition of brother/sisterhood, and our unity as Spirit.

But many people are so emotionally attached that they fear or worry about what their animals could communicate to them. Their conception and demonstration of love is mixed with emotional dependency, sympathy in the form of pity, or a condescending view of animals as poor underlings. Panicky clinging and smothering with attention or affection can demean animals and prevent them from being themselves and growing. These are among the surest blocks to clear reception of what others are really thinking and feeling. All you get back are your own fixated or uncleared emotional reactions.

This dark side or neurotic aspect of "love" can make it impossible for people to accept their animal companions as independent agents: spirits who have their own feelings, thoughts, and responsibility for their own lives. So, these people aren't quite able to consider that animals have minds of their own, or that they can make a telepathic connection with them.

It may take a lot of soul searching, counseling, and inner work to get through these attitudes, to create a more balanced relationship with others in one's life. If you are going to help others through interspecies telepathic communication, it is necessary to grow into emotional and spiritual adulthood with regard to knowing yourself as a whole being. Then you can allow that maturity to manifest in the animals you meet, also.

On the other hand, you can't be coldly detached, unsympathetic, or insensitive. You need to feel love for others in the form of respect, acceptance, kindness, and consideration, so that you can interpret and handle the communication you receive with balance, compassion, and wisdom.

I find that most people who truly love animals are very considerate and open to the rest of the world. However, many animal people mention that they are able to relate better to animals than to people, or that they don't really like or feel comfortable with people.

It is hardest to love those who reflect, most accurately, our own unresolved issues. When we see our faults, challenges, problems, and conflicts mirrored in other humans, we may criticize, feel uncomfortable, or want to reject these people and find someone to relate to who does not arouse these feelings. The irony is that animals often take on and mirror our faults or dis-ease, or we attract those beings in animal form that have the same issues to deal with as we do. We may end up resenting or feeling uncomfortable with these animals, until we are willing to help each other to face and resolve or heal these issues.

One of humanity's greatest challenges is to respect, accept, feel compassion for—to love—one another. As you learn about tele-pathic communication and deepen your connection with animals, you may find this capacity brings self-knowledge and understand-ing and even more compassion for our fellow humans.

It also appears that telepathic development is not a matter of developing some new power through mental exercises. It is more a matter of opening up to love.

Kate Solisti-Mattelon tells about her heart opening reconnec-tion with animals:

As a young child I heard the plants, animals, and minerals speaking to me. I thought everybody could hear them; I quickly learned that this was not the case. Hearing over and over, "It's just your imagination, Dear," made me doubt the truth of my deeper connection. In order to be "accepted" by family and friends, I "shut down" my ability to hear. I tried to forget what I had heard, but somehow always remembered conversations with my cat.

As an adult I longed to "hear" my animal friends again, but I had no idea how to reawaken this ability. A friend told me about Penelope. I sent immediately for her book, *Animal Talk*, and devoured it. I thought, "If she can do it, I can too, I think." At this point I realized that animal communication is a matter of the heart.

I began working on my own, removing the emotional blocks that I knew were preventing me from being open. All of those years of people telling me, "You can't," "That's impossible," and "Don't be ridiculous," took some time to erase. As we entered our thirties, my husband and I began personal growth work to heal our marriage—another matter of the heart. We spent seven intensive months removing anger, emotional pain, and old belief systems. Our lives and marriage improved greatly. Happiness, once so elusive, became a reality.

In January of 1992, while taking a course in Reiki healing, I met a professional psychic who invited me to become his apprentice. I was flabbergasted! Apparently, my personal growth work had resulted in a reawakening of my psychic abilities. As we worked together, I was amazed at what I could sense. I allowed myself to receive details of his mother's childhood and origins of his favorite crystals. Then I opened a strong connection with my own spirit guide. Finally, my friend and teacher asked me, "What do you want to do with your abilities?" I responded, "I want to hear animals and plants again." My husband and he had given me the support and encouragement that I needed; now it was time to go do it!

He sent me to one of his own clients to help her figure out what was wrong with her golden retriever. To my delight, I was able to hear the dog, who shared with me a traumatic event from his past. I described it to his person, and all the pieces fell together for them both. The dog forgave her instantly, once the misunderstanding was cleared up. His health steadily improved from that point on. Wow, I was doing it! I was communicating! Now what?

In order to practice my reawakened ability, I decided to volunteer at my veterinarian's clinic. I practiced Reiki healing and animal communication with recovering animals. For me this turned out to be fabulous practice. The animals really wanted someone to talk to, so I listened, I reassured them, and I helped them physically with Reiki. My confidence grew, and the work expanded. Soon pet owners began to call me. Word spread, and I was featured in a statewide Sunday newspaper. Now I am pursuing animal communication full time. I am happier than I had ever been, and I learn more with each conversation.

If I can do it, YOU CAN DO IT. Be patient, practice listening, and clear out the emotional blocks. With a strong commitment, you'll reawaken in your own time and in your own way. Trust the process. Soon you'll become a link to the past and a powerful influence on the future as you help animals and people understand each other.

Jeri Ryan relates an experience that illustrates the role of love, and faith in miracles:

I always call upon St. Francis of Assisi to assist me in my communications with animals and to assist them in whatever way they need.

One day, while completing a psychotherapy session with a human, I received a desperate phone call from a woman with a life-and-death matter. Her sealed skylight was inviting a trapped and very frantic hummingbird to apparent freedom, all the while presenting an invisible barrier. The woman had unsuccessfully attempted to guide the little bird to an open window.

She was a young bird, very disoriented, and hardly noticed my telepathic calling. She tuned in briefly to me, taking only the time to show me her frightened self, and then she continued her frantic treadmill search for an escape.

I felt hopeless and impotent. In spite of the creeping self-doubts, I made one last attempt by calling on St. Francis and anyone out there to show this little bird the way to safety and freedom.

At that point, the process was interrupted by the arrival of my next human client. I was afraid to call the hummingbird person back, certain that the little bird had died from exhaustion, or smashed herself against the skylight.

However, she called to report that the hummingbird had stopped and suddenly changed her course just before

I hung up the phone on the previous call, and that she left through an open window immediately after we hung up. With some awe, she also reported that it looked as though she had been carried by invisible hands down to the open window.

I too am in awe. I hadn't told her that I asked St. Francis to do that very thing. The gift for me is one of trust and of faith in the guidance of the universe, in this process of universal telepathic communication, and in myself. An added gift, not insignificant, is a belief in the miracles of the universe, which may be more commonplace than is generally expected.

POINTERS TO ENHANCE TELEPATHIC COMMUNICATION

The following pointers are designed to help you become and remain receptive to telepathic communication with animals. Use these tips to move yourself through communication blocks and to increase your potential as you practice the steps in the next chapter.

1. *More than any other factor, your attitude toward animals* influences how receptive you are to their communication and how willing they may be to communicate with you.

Respect and revere animals as fellow beings—different in physical form than you but of the same spiritual essence and potential.

If you approach animals with condescension, thinking they are inferior in intelligence or awareness, or substandard in any way, you limit your ability to perceive and understand them as they truly are. As you increasingly see and treat them as fellow intelligent beings, you allow them to express themselves more deeply and fully to you, and your relationship develops, matures, elevates, and expands.

Focusing only on the biological aspect of an animal, while fascinating and wondrous in itself, can place you in the rut of conventional notions of popular psychology and inhibit perception of the true spiritual essence and wisdom behind the physical form.

Admiring an animal's spiritual qualities—such as sincerity, trust, love, devotion, appreciation, loyalty, empathy, kindness, honor, honesty, patience, integrity, humility, joy, unselfishness, wisdom—will help to transform your whole relationship, enhancing the two-way communication and understanding between you.

Be humble and receptive, and allow animals to teach you.

2. *Believe in your own intuitive ability* to give and receive telepathic communication. Don't invalidate your perception of impressions, images, or messages in any form.

3. *Be ready, receptive, mentally quiet, and alert.* If your mind is busy, full of thoughts and background static, you can't listen and receive.

Attaining the receptive state may take considerable practice and changes in lifestyle. Avoid substances and environmental conditions that dull the mind or make it too agitated. Adopt habits that reduce stress and increase calmness, including a balanced whole-food diet, exercise and rest, yoga, meditation, spending quiet time with your animal friends, and communing with nature.

4. *Cultivate flexibility*—that is, a willingness to learn from all beings and to change your ideas. Watch for judgments and preconceptions that limit receptivity to what the animal is really communicating. *Be open to surprises; welcome the unexpected.* Let go of conventional notions of human–animal communication.

Be ready for animals to communicate, and question them on any level—from what food they like, to what they might teach to improve your life, to what they consider the most profound truths.

5. *Be emotionally peaceful.* Having an emotional investment in what animals say to you or how they should be can influence what you receive. If you require that animals like you or be affectionate before you can communicate with them, this can disturb them, block their true feelings, or cloud your receptiveness to them.

In working to improve your two-way communication with animals, don't flood animals with emotion, whether love, fear, sadness, or anger. If you are conveying a strong emotion, you are generally not receptive to anything else, and you will get back only your own emotion or the animal's response to it.

6. *Be alert and calm.* Don't force the communication or try too hard. Notice your body posture and tension—leaning forward over the animal, straining the forehead or facial muscles, breathing shallowly, tightening hands, or moving to manipulate or control the animal.

Shift into the receptive mode. Lean back, open your chest and hands, breathe slowly and deeply, relax, and listen.

7. *Let communication assume its own form*, whether it be feelings, images, impressions, thoughts, verbal messages, sounds, other sensations, or simply knowing. Become familiar with your manner of receiving, so that you may recognize and allow it and open up to yet other avenues of receptivity.

Let the sense of meaning unfold by itself. Don't analyze, evaluate, or criticize. Remain innocent and nonjudgmental. Accept what you get, and acknowledge the communication. If in doubt, relax, and ask again, but don't continue to doubt or refuse to accept a communication impression, for such resistance leads to building your own walls.

Be willing to take risks—don't be afraid to acknowledge whatever communication you get. Don't worry about what other people will think or even what you will think!

8. *Practice with a wide variety of animals* in various situations. Step back from your normal routine and expectations, and be willing to learn and discover.

Have fun!

HOW TO

communicate

WITH animals –

STEP BY STEP

WHAT TECHNIQUES CAN WE practice to regain the ability to communicate telepathically with animals, both on the giving and receiving ends?

In my workshops, people practice with their animal companions, using the steps outlined below. No one becomes an expert at the end of one workshop or practice session. Expertise requires a lot of sensitivity and experience. Some people become acutely aware of how they are blocking themselves from understanding animals and recognizing what they need to work on. This is an important step to getting in touch with one's innate ability. Most people proceed to gain more awareness and certainty about their ability, which increases as they practice the communication techniques in their daily living.

If you do the following exercises well, with a patient attitude, allowing your perceptions to unfold, you may have some interesting and even exciting results.

STEP 1: OBSERVING QUIETLY

One of the major barriers to receiving communication from animals is allowing the interference of your own thoughts, distractions, or preconceived notions. You need to be quietly receptive to what animals wish to relay. If you add to or change their communication, you won't really understand them.

The first step in overcoming this habit is to find a time when you and an animal friend can be together in a peaceful environment. Sit comfortably within a few feet of each other, or whatever distance is agreeable to the animal. Don't try to grasp for attention or do anything that might be distracting. Just look at the animal quietly. Let all distractions, thoughts, or images of other things melt away, and focus softly on the animal. Continue to do this until you feel very relaxed and calm, with a relatively clear mind.

After doing this awhile, you probably will have experienced heightened awareness or clearer perceptions about yourself and animals. It may have been a relief to calm down and let busy thoughts fade away.

You should now feel better about being calm, close, and sympathetic with your animal friend. You may wish to repeat this step with other animals.

You may at first, or even with repeated practice, only experience your own mental activity. You may find you cannot calm the million thoughts and images that crowd your mind. Or you receive no fresh observations or perceptions about the animal. You may get fixated on the animal's body and cannot get beyond this to be aware of their whole being. You may not yet perceive their spiritual essence, their thoughts, feelings, or concepts of who they are on a deeper level— all the myriad aspects of their being that might be contacted.

Be patient. Increased awareness and telepathic reception take time to cultivate. This is not a recipe for instant mashed potatoes! For many people, years of "rust" or blocks have accumulated. Continued practice helps the layers to peel away.

As you practice this frequently, you will find your own judgments or accumulated preconceptions about animals coming into view. Be willing to let them go, and open up to fresh observations based on a clear connection to the animal present with you. You will then find that your receptivity to animals' thoughts, feelings, concepts, and images increases.

Remember that this is the first and most basic step that must be realized for further communication to take place. It is what makes it safe for an animal (human or otherwise) to open up to you and feel that you are listening and can understand. Do it daily—or whenever needed, for minutes or hours—with people, animals, trees, rocks, or whomever you wish to sense with deeper understanding and connection.

As you go on to the next steps, be sure to have this step in place as your foundation.

STEP 2: DELIVERING THE MESSAGE

ATTENTION

People have asked me why their animal friends don't appear to respond to them when the people attempt to communicate. The animals don't seem to get it. What's wrong?

There can be several things incorrect with the way you're sending the message. Did you ever ask someone a question when the respondent's mind was on something else, so that you were heard only vaguely, if at all? The same thing can happen in communicating with animals.

You need to have their attention, their willingness, and their ability to listen to you. Sometimes, all it takes is calling their name and they're all eyes and ears for you. With others, a friendly tap or rub to let them know you're there is what's needed before you speak to them. Often animals will direct their attention to you if you're simply quiet and attentive, as in the basic observation exercise.

While in many instances animals will look at you to let you know they're listening, this is not always their preference. I've noticed with many animals that we can hold great conversations while their eyes are directed toward their environment, alert to their surroundings, as is their nature.

What is necessary is your feeling that they are listening to you. People normally can sense if others are "with" them or elsewhere mentally. If your intention to communicate with them is calm and clear, and you put that across, there should be no problem.

The only time I require that animals look at me directly while I'm talking to them is when we're correcting some behavior and/or the animals have deliberately resisted listening, and it's important that they get what I'm saying. For example, when my dogs have misbehaved, I'll hold their faces toward me to emphasize the point.

Once you're really calmly being with animals, it's easy to perceive when they're ready and willing to listen. Obviously, you don't try to deliver your communication when animals are distracted by food, other animals, or noises. First handle the distraction, and then get focused or attentive together.

CLARITY

The next element is how you deliver your message. Whether spoken or silent, it must be clear to really get across. Ensure that the message is not muddled with other thoughts or mental images.

An example of this is when people are trying to teach dogs simple obedience commands. People will say "come" to their dogs, but will picture mentally that the dogs are going to run away from them. The animals will usually get the person's initial intention to come, but the pictures of running away can confuse them. So, they either hesitate, or follow the mental images and run away, thinking that's what the person wants them to do.

Remember that animals pick up the thoughts or meaning behind the words and learn to associate the words with the action you are picturing. Don't confuse them. Keep your meaning or picture matched with what you are asking or saying. The thought, image, or feeling you project while you use words is more important than the words themselves. That's why animals can usually spot insincere people, because what the people are saying is not what they are thinking or feeling, and animals get the thought or feeling and act accordingly.

I have found that some animals who could never be taught commands, or who seemed not to listen to what their person wanted, were quite agreeable to listen or train after their previous confusion about what their people really meant was cleared up.

Be clear mentally when you speak. Mean what you say. Sound adds an attention-getting and attention-holding dimension. Communicating your thoughts aloud verbally can be more effective, since we're all accustomed to it. However, when you are close to certain animals who trust you and are really listening, silent communication can be wonderful. I often talk aloud with my own animal family. They enjoy hearing my voice, and I enjoy conversing with them that way. Sound helps to emphasize any instructions I need to give. When I do a consultation, most of it is nonverbal, as we can communicate about problems and counsel traumatic experiences more easily and quickly that way.

Holding or touching animals sensitively while you talk can also add more receptivity to your communications. Physical contact helps to keep them there if they are tempted not to face something you need to deal with, or they're having a hard time telling you about something. It lets them know you are confident and in control, when needed, and that you have a desire to be close to them. This can add to the understanding of your communication.

THE PROCEDURE

Let's break this down step by step for you to practice:

1. Visualize something. Simply practice creating a mental picture of some object or scene and look at it mentally. This is something we do naturally and almost constantly, so it should be easy.

2. Visualize something and send it to the air a few feet in front of your body. You can project it there, like tossing a ball, or just decide to have it appear in that place. Your mental images are under your command.

3. Visualize something and send it to a specific point in the room—e.g., the wall or the bookshelf.

4. Visualize something and send it to your animal friend's body. Be confident your picture will arrive there. You can also verbalize what you picture as you send it. Practice both silently and verbally.

5. Get your animal friend's attention. Call her name or rub her back, or focus intently on her to let her know you're there and wish to communicate.

6. Say hello. Ensure that she got it. Repeat if necessary.

7. Picture a simple wish or an image your animal friend might be interested in (e.g., a loved one or a walk on the beach), match your words to the thought, and send the message to the animal. Repeat this process until you feel good about doing it and sense that you are getting across. (Caution: Don't overdo the same images, as the animal may get bored and tune out.)

Conscious effort to mentally visualize what you verbalize is not necessary, once you've practiced this technique and are sure you can mean what you say. Word and image can occur simultaneously, naturally. Don't overdo this or make it difficult.

Review this step to recognize likely pitfalls of delivering a message, and correct your own procedure if necessary.

That's fairly easy, isn't it? Yes, you say, but how do I know my animal friends got the message? What about their answer? The next step: consider the animal's response.

STEP 3: RECEIVING AN ANSWER

This is the part that most people feel uncertain about. They may think getting the communication to the animal is easy, but they don't get anything back, or do they?

A lot depends on how well you are applying the first step. Are you observing calmly, perceiving clearly, and listening to the animal, or are you thinking, thinking, thinking, and rummaging over all the things you think the animal might or should say? On this will depend whether your channel is open to get the message.

Of course, if you've given a command, it's easy to see the animal's answer in the physical response. How about if you ask a question? How do you know you've received an answer?

IMAGINATION

Let's do a little preparation by working with imagination. The word *imagine* comes from "imago," an image or likeness, and means "to make a mental image of, form an idea or notion of; conceive in the mind." Imagination is commonly regarded as a fanciful thing, creating things that are not "real" or present in the physical realm. It is often derided, as in the suggestion, "It's just your imagination."

However, without the ability to imagine, a person would not be able to proceed with a plan of action or perceive others' communications. If you can't imagine, or create a mental image of something, you often can't see or hear or sense it in other ways. It literally may not exist for you, as in the statement, "I just can't imagine that." Obviously, if you can't imagine receiving communication from an animal (or anyone), you won't be able to receive it. Receiving mental images and thoughts requires the ability to create them for yourself and perceive that they exist.

Let's get some practice:

1. With your animal friend near you, get his attention. Say "hello," and *imagine* he says "hello" back to you. You don't actually have to receive a response on this step. You're basically opening up to the idea and flow of receiving communication back from your animal friend.

Imagine hearing the "hello" response. Practice this until you are certain you can imagine it. You may even find that your animal companion answers you, or you may perceive that he is sending you a greeting in response. Just practice, and get the idea of receiving a flow of communication, by allowing it to come back to you. Use the power of your imagination. Form the mental image and perceive the "hello" or greeting coming back.

Practice this with a number of animals, if you wish, before going on to the next step.

2. Now, with your willingness and ability to receive mental communication wide open, get your animal friend's attention (if you don't already have it) and ask the very simple question, "How are you doing?"

3. *Listen, and accept what you get.*

Thoughts are instantaneous. They don't take long to travel the distance. They don't necessarily come packaged as words. You may receive the answer as an idea, concept, impression, image, or feeling perception. Take it.

People are better at picking up the thoughts and feelings of the animals and people to whom they are close than they give themselves credit for. A major barrier to receiving communication is invalidating what you perceive or doubting your own ability to make contact. Take my word for it: You have the ability. Practice, and build your own confidence.

Many times during a consultation, I will explain to people what the animal relates about something, and they'll respond, "I thought she was trying to say that," or "I picked up something like that."

Instead of trusting their perceptions and acknowledging the messages they have received from their animal friends, they have doubted the connection and so been unable to fully understand what's happening. Just pointing out to people that they are doing this, often helps to increase their perception and confidence on the spot.

Instead of allowing yourself to think you can't do it, trust that you have the ability, and accept whatever communication you immediately receive. Practice will improve your quality or clarity of perception.

Don't worry if your perceptions don't always seem to correspond with accepted notions of reality or agree with other people's ideas. You need to start to validate your own perceptions. As you continue to practice, your accuracy and ability to comprehend what you perceive will improve. Moreover, as you learn to accept the communications you get, notice how your relationships with animals improve.

In a troubled situation, it helps to have a person who is not emotionally involved to help sort things out. Emotional upset can be a barrier to mental reception. If I get excited or upset, as when my dog has wandered far on a mountain trail and not returned for awhile, I'm lucky if I can see ten feet in front of my body, much less get in touch with my dog and perceive his location. So, one needs to remain or become calm.

Be willing to accept whatever thought or mental picture or emotion your animal friend gives, in answer to your question. Adding your own thoughts will make it difficult for you. For example, you ask your dog how she is doing, and the immediate thought you receive is "miserable." Instead of taking that communication from her as it is, you look at her and think, "No, she couldn't have thought that; she looks fine, her coat is shiny, I feed her well, so she must be okay." You have just added your own thoughts or images to the answer, so you negate her communication and your ability to receive further messages.

Most animal companions will try to get across to you again if you ask and really want to hear their answer. However, much like human companions, they can give up and figure you're not really interested if you continue to add your own interpretations. Most animals who love you will be thrilled that you want to listen to what they have to say, and they will brighten up immensely when you start to work with them.

If they refuse to answer and don't seem to want to listen to you in the first place, they may have some cause for upset with you, perhaps a longstanding cause. They may not immediately tune into you and cooperate, after being tuned out for a long time. Animals, like people, learn to behave according to what is expected. They may not respond to a sudden reversal of expectations.

Keep trying, and give them a chance to respond to you. You may be pleasantly surprised. Communication, if sincerely continued, can melt all resistance. The reward is an enriched relationship for both of you, as long as the next, very important step is followed.

4. Acknowledge whatever animals communicate. Smile, say "thanks" or "okay," or give a friendly pat, and let your animal friends know you received what they said.

Don't just sit there puzzling over what you perceived as the answer. Acknowledgment is an important part of communication. It lets you and the animal know you were listening and understood as best you could.

5. If you didn't get what your animal friends communicated, it's all right to ask the same question again. It's also fine to ask other questions that help you to clarify what you understood as their response.

In human conversations we sometimes don't hear or understand what the speaker is saying and need to ask again. If you've arrived this far, your animal companions will probably be quite willing to answer again or elaborate. It doesn't hurt to ask.

6. If your animal helpers happen to relay something else that's bothering them, or if they want to communicate something unrelated to your question or topic, be sure to accept and understand it and act accordingly. Acknowledge them thoroughly, and then get back to the original question or topic.

They may suddenly think of something they've wanted to tell you for years. Don't slight it or think they're evading the question, as this will seldom be the case. Even if they are avoiding your question, don't get upset, but handle whatever they say with consideration. Then you may return to your original topic. If you resolve what is distracting the animal, you'll increase harmony in both of your lives.

7. Once you are satisfied with an answer to the first question, ask another, such as: "Is there anything you want to tell me?"

Apply all the prior steps. Practice this with your own or other animal companions. It will get easier. You'll find that different animals, like different humans, respond in varied ways. Some have a lot to say; some say very little. Some will be quite cheerful, others sad or bored. Accept what you receive, no matter how different it seems from your expectations.

Some animals clearly let you know what they want or how they feel by their physical actions. Observing their body language and matching it to the telepathic communication can contribute to increased accuracy of understanding. However, when you get into telepathic conversations, don't expect continual outward expressions. Both of you may get very calm when the ready communion of direct thought and feeling perception gets going. There is often no need for excessive physical display when you both fully understand each other. I often do whole consultations with animals resting quietly, apparently not paying attention, but we are deeply in touch with each other.

Another way of increasing willingness to communicate and adding new dimensions of loving understanding is to send admiration and appreciation to animals. Simply sit calmly, and admire all the beautiful qualities, physical and spiritual, that you can find about the animal. You can also verbalize your feelings of appreciation and respect on a daily basis. Your mutual trust and affection will grow. That's what we're aiming for. You can't lose. So, practice, practice, practice with as many domestic and wild animals as possible, and have loads of fun!

SUMMARY OF STEPS

Here's a brief recap of the main steps for your ease of practice:

1. Quietly observe your animal friend while letting your own mind grow calm, and become open to perceive and receive clearly.

2. Visualize something, and practice sending the image to specific places, including your animal friend's body.

3. Get your animal friend's attention, and send a hello or other message or image.

4. Say "hello," and imagine your animal friend is saying "hello" back to you.

5. Ask a question, and accept whatever communication you receive from your animal companion.

6. Acknowledge the answer.

7. Practice with other questions and other animals.

Enjoy yourself!

KEEP IT SIMPLE

Telepathic communication with our fellow animals is so natural and easy that we may miss it by looking for something more difficult. Communication with animals is just like having a conversation with another person. Sometimes you don't understand what the animal is communicating, or you only get part of it and later fill in the details and come to understand more fully, just as in human conversations. As you become a better listener and more fully comprehend how you receive telepathically, it becomes quicker and easier to get the full message the animal is relaying. As with any other skill, you improve with practice.

Watch for underlying cultural programming that suggests animals are not intelligent or are less intelligent and couldn't possibly communicate, or that they are aware of only rudimentary things or a limited environment. These ideas will hinder you from receiving what animals communicate and from believing what you receive. You may color their communications with a feeling that an animal couldn't possibly have a particular thought—e.g., that a "pig" or "dog" is limited to certain thoughts. Let them educate you. Believe the images, thoughts, impressions, and words that you receive from them. Acknowledge each communication received, and you will continue to expand.

Even if you make mistakes and don't always understand correctly, don't despair! Don't we do that in human communication? But take courage: Telepathic communication is so direct in impact of feeling and concept that it may be even less subject to misinterpretation than verbal language.

We always add our own flavor to whatever we receive. The clearest communicators are those who add the least of their own agendas. They put themselves aside to be good listeners, to let the message flow, and to express through the medium of human language with the least alteration and the most feeling and intention from the animal. You can't receive another's thoughts and feelings clearly and consistently unless your own channel is clear and you are mentally flexible and receptive.

PROOF

The results speak for themselves. If the beings involved get more upset and confused and don't change for the better, then your interpretations were off the mark. If more harmony, cooperation, relaxation, and happiness result, you emulated the communication well, so that there was room for positive change to take place.

The animals are eager for you to be receptive to their communication. As you practice, their response to your telepathic understanding of them will let you know whether you are on the right track or not. When you receive communication well and acknowledge it, there is a sense of truth, compassion, and understanding that brings about the other's cooperation.

This is not a laboratory experiment that can be closed off from the rest of life and repeated over and over to get the same results. Communication and understanding among beings is a fluid and ever-changing phenomenon. Proof of the effectiveness of communication is gathered as animals change their behavior, and all those involved become happier, healthier, and more harmonious.

Learn to trust, to take the plunge. Don't label the results of communication as coincidence, or try to confine them into neat behavioral, "scientific" explanations. Learn to experience with your whole being—your feelings and all your senses, through your whole body, not just with the analytical functioning of the mind— so you can accept and *know* what you perceive. Open to fullness with your whole heart, both sides of your brain, your whole body, and your total spirit. You'll understand and grow, and others around you will flourish.

The following is an example of how telepathic communication works, even if you don't believe in it. Sometimes people will not credit what they see, or they will explain it away as coincidence or random chance. In the following instance, the person noticed what happened.

Early one December, a man was cleaning the chicken coop and getting it ready for winter. He had two hens and one rooster. The hens hadn't laid any eggs for about a month, so he began telling them that after all this work and feeding them every day, he expected an egg apiece by Christmas to show their appreciation. Otherwise, he said to them, a stuffed chicken dinner might be nice for Christmas.

He was only joking and forgot about what he had said to them until Christmas morning when he went out to the chicken coop. There in the nest box were two eggs—the first eggs in almost two months.

He was a bit shocked and looked around for human tracks in the snow to see if someone was playing a joke on him, but the fresh snow cover showed no such evidence.

The hens kept on laying eggs regularly after that.

BECOMING THE ANIMAL

Another way to fully experience communication and understanding with animals is to become them—to step inside their viewpoints, to see things through their eyes, hear things through their ears, smell through their noses, feel and think through their bodies and minds. This is the most direct form of communication, without translation needed—a total being and feeling of oneness.

Try the following exercise by reading it to a friend or taping it and gently following along while, or after, you read the instructions. You may find that each time you practice this exercise, you improve your ability to fully assume an animal's viewpoint and understand their perspectives directly.

MEDITATION ON BECOMING AN ANIMAL

We're going to do a meditation exercise on becoming an animal, so you can get a different perspective on communicating with animals.

Sit with your feet flat on the floor and your spine as erect as is comfortable. Close your eyes. Take a deep breath and slowly let it out. Continue breathing deeply and slowly, relaxing and being here comfortably, in mind and body. Let any tension you feel in your body—neck, head, chest, etc.—be released through you and into the ground, as you exhale. Continue to breathe deeply and let go of any physical or mental distractions. Feel yourself centered, grounded, calm in body and mind. If at any time during the exercise you feel distracted or confused, breathe slowly and deeply, then continue.

Be receptive and childlike, letting yourself move fully into visualizing and sensing. Choose an animal or let one appear to help you. Imagine clearly and notice its physical features. Notice something you've never noticed before about it. Notice something else you hadn't noticed before.

Sense the animal's mental and spiritual qualities, its thoughts and its essence as a being. Feel in close contact with it. Notice the animal's breathing, and synchronize your own breath with the animal. As you inhale and exhale in rhythm with the animal, let yourself make a gradual shift until you are inside the animal's viewpoint.

See things through its eyes. Feel your feet on the ground, or your body in contact with your environment. Notice how the body and body parts feel—legs or other appendages, head, skin, fur. Notice your height, weight, the temperature and texture of your body.

Move around in your animal body. Notice how you move, how it feels. As that animal, go to your favorite environment. How do you feel? What do you like to do? What are you interested in?

Express emotions through your animal body (sadness, fear, anger, boredom, and joy). How do you do that? Through your animal form, experience how it feels to sense, smell, see, hear, touch, taste, and think. (Take time on each.)

Meet another animal of your type, and yet another. What is your response? Approach an area where there are humans, or notice a few humans approaching your environment. How do you feel about them? Establish any contact with them that is comfortable for you.

How do you perceive their thoughts, emotions, intentions, and actions? How do they feel toward you? Ask a question, or try to get something you want from a human. How do you do that? Do they understand you? What do they do?

How are you different from humans? How are you similar? What things are most important to you? What games do you like to play? How does being this animal compare to being human? Does your body influence the way you act, react, think, feel, and live? How do you feel about yourself?

Go back to your favorite environment alone. Fully experience enjoying your animal body. Relax, eat, rest, be alert, and play. Do something you really like to do as that animal.

Being aware of your own breathing, slowly shift yourself from your animal form, back to your current human viewpoint, looking at the animal body. Notice how you feel about that animal now.

When you're ready, open your eyes, return your awareness to the physical surroundings, look around, stretch, and smile!

BREAKTHROUGHS

Recovering the ability to telepathically communicate with animals may still seem difficult for you. Here are some of the barriers that people have encountered along the way and how they have broken through them:

> I seem to have a greater facility in communicating with one dog over another. I think that my biggest problem is emptying my head of spurious thoughts long enough for theirs to reach me. Being still, unfortunately, has never been one of my strong suits.

> I've been working at hearing my animal teachers, but could never quite "get it." I knew they were trying to get through my "thick skull," but I couldn't quite figure it out. Your encouragement to acknowledge and validate really has helped.

I have great news: since the workshop I've been able to communicate with animals. At first, it came as a total surprise. I guess the two days simply allowed the door to open up and to trust my antennas. I also attribute this discovery to my long experience as a therapist and patient. The listening (receptive) attitude is similar.

So, it is a matter of switching channels. Anyway, I'm doing it, with my animals and a few others I meet along the way. Thank you from deep in my heart for facilitating this fascinating and still troubling discovery. My whole perception of animals and relationship with them has changed. An unspeakable gift.

Others report the transformative power of direct telepathic communication with their animal companions after doing a workshop:

I realized that animals love to play, to make us happy and light, but I needed to be reminded to treat them as wise and intelligent beings, not just as cute and cuddly "pets."

The workshop was like looking through a door of possibilities, where you could peek through and get a glimpse of what really can be. It was awesome, frightening, titillating, exciting.

Humans, because of generations of conditioning, just don't believe that this hocus-pocus "telepathy stuff" was really ever accessible to them. Penelope's workshop helps you do what you know instinctively can be done. It was so much fun.

Not only did the workshop help increase my confidence and ability to communicate with animals. I also already feel I communicate better with other people and other life forms. It's really exciting.

The workshop made me grateful to animals for living with us!

Can you imagine what it's like to become a frog . . . to swim across a backyard pond, to squat on a lily pad, to eat an insect, to watch humans enjoying you enjoying yourself? I did this and much more while reawakening my ability to telepathically communicate with the animals in the workshop. It was truly magical.

The workshop made me aware of how much communication I was already receiving. It wasn't just my mind wandering. I learned how to direct communication back and to seek it out instead of randomly receiving it.

The workshop encouraged me to quiet myself and hear the animals around me.

After the workshop, I was playing with a stray cat. When I said, "Hey, that hurts," she retracted her claws. A horse at a distance turned to look at me every time I wished I could talk to him. Many similar incidents have enlightened and encouraged me as I discover this "new" way to communicate.

I get the feeling now that all my animal friends expect me to understand them better now. I understand more of who they really are, and I'm having more fun, and I think they are with me, too. The first week after the workshop, I was so "high" with energy and happiness that by the following weekend I was tired from being so happy!

At the beginning of the first workshop exercise of the day, I became aware that the chatter of parrots, barks and yips of dogs, and movements of mouse, ferret, and cat were no longer there. In that absolute silence and stillness of humans and animals joined in purpose was an energy I had never felt before, and I entered a different state of awareness. All separation of bodies and forms disappeared, and I knew our oneness, that we were all part of the same consciousness, that there were no differences in our essential beings. It was a fleeting knowledge of what really is, and a great joy and peace filled me.

To say that your seminar was life-changing for me is an understatement! I had no idea that my animals would have so much to say to me when I got home . . . but, boy, was I in for a surprise.

How valuable this workshop was for me. It goes far beyond telepathy. For me it was a further in-depth reconnection with the universe and with myself.

Full Moon Anima

From where does this telepathic communication come?
From that body? Doesn't seem to.
Attentive, asleep? Even there?
To whom does it matter?
How big is the soul?
If we contact their soul across space and time
where are we? And when?

"Innocence" you whisper mentally.

To hear what another has to say
we seem to have to hear
what our soul has to say.
Open to another and you're open to yourself.
Gotcha!
To hear their truth, we must hear our truth.
Ha! A wonderful technique.

A smile the most you say.

Out of the timeless giant pool of knowingness
seems to come whatever comes.

Keep on.

Keep on.

—Roy Poucher

Opening up to telepathic communication with other species is a path of opening to who you are as a being. It's a path of self-discovery as well as universal connection. Enjoy the journey!

SHOWING

THAT THEY

understand

You MAY STILL WONDER how you will know that telepathic communication is happening, that the animals understand and that you are indeed receiving the animals' messages correctly.

Remember to honor that the animals can understand you, that they can get the thoughts, meaning, feelings, and intentions behind your words. With this respect for their intelligence, they are more likely to respond to you and show you that they understand, for your benefit and for theirs. Also honor that you, too, as a fellow spiritual being, are able to receive and understand others' communication. Here's an example:

Sherry returned home from a ride on her newly acquired Arabian stallion. She took his saddle off and put it away, and he wandered over to play with his mare. The horse showed no interest in coming to Sherry when she called him. So she mentally projected a picture of him turning around, walking to her, lowering his head, and her taking off his bridle. His head went up, he looked at her with great surprise, and did just that. He had never come across a human who tried to communicate with him that way.

DOG OBEDIENCE WITH A NEW TWIST

Understanding does not necessarily equate with obedience. This is a common human assumption—that if animals understand people, they will do what people want. If they don't obey, they're considered by many people to be stupid and incapable of comprehending.

People, especially those involved in training animals, sometimes ask me if my dogs are very obedient, since I can communicate with them directly. No, they are not the classically trained, obedient dogs. I don't expect them to be. We work things out together and make agreements on what's beneficial for all of us, given our needs and the requirements of human society around us. Intelligent understanding of another's communication in any species may bring about the opposite of obedience if they don't see a good reason to obey!

When Pasha arrived in my life on February 24, 1979, as a six-month-old Afghan puppy, I was thrilled with his playful exuberance, self-confidence, friendliness with everyone, and general zest for adventure. He was eight months old when we began a six-month tour around the country with my older Afghan, Popiya, in a 1964 Dodge van I called Pegasus.

We traveled from the West Coast beaches through the Rocky Mountains to the New England shore, and wherever we went, I tried to find wilderness or park areas where the dogs could run freely and safely. Popiya usually did not wander far and returned to me in a short time. Pasha, my born-free puppy, raced for hours, chasing seagulls and squirrels. I had little control of when he would return. Obedience to commands was not established in our repertoire. I just enjoyed his spirit of freedom and knew he would return when he was ready. When I called or visualized him returning, eventually he would pay attention and come back to the van.

This laissez-faire coexistence worked well for us, as I enjoyed his zest for life, and I didn't have any pressure to make things different. One time when we were visiting someone's house, Pasha jumped on a woman in his friendly way, and she objected. She was a dog trainer, and said, "Well, you certainly haven't done any obedience training with him, have you?"

I had to examine my feelings about that. As soon as she said "obedience training," I thought of bondage, a master–slave relationship between human and dog. I resisted the notion. I felt Pasha wasn't harming anyone, and we enjoyed life together as it was. I also saw her point. He didn't have the dog manners that human society required, and I had little control over his actions.

So, when we returned from our tour, and Pasha was fourteen months old, I told him we would need to do obedience training, so that he would develop manners with which people could be comfortable. I'm a do-it-yourselfer, so I read books on obedience and commenced lessons at home. I didn't do it in the rote, repetitive, choke-chain method most trainers recommended at the time. I just explained to Pasha what I wanted him to do and used the word commands and hand signals to direct him to do it.

In two days of several fifteen-minute sessions, Pasha had mastered the basic "sit," "stay," "down," "down-stay," even to the extent of having a piece of cheese on his nose while I left the room, to return and find he had left it there as I told him to. This is miraculous for a dog who had always been a chowhound!

After performing these commands perfectly in two days, Pasha asked me, "Okay, is that enough of this stuff, now?" I told him that it would be enough of obedience training as long as he would sit and stay when other people and I needed that of him. I told him he would have to watch people and be attentive to their thoughts and feelings and apply dog manners accordingly.

He loved lightly jumping up on people and laying those big Afghan paws on their shoulders as he greeted them. I told them he could still do that, if people liked it and thought it was fun. For those that did not like it, he was to sit and wait for their greeting and not jump up. He rarely misjudged and was mannerly whenever it was really required, although he loved to stretch people to laugh and lighten up with his charming antics. Most people adored him.

Coming when called was another matter. Afghans are sight hounds—born to run for miles and hunt by sight rather than with nose to the ground. To most Afghans, the word *come* means "see you later." We worked on "come" for weeks, with meager results. It was not a command that seemed reasonable to Pasha.

Since I let Pasha run free daily, there were obvious dangers in racing out of sight, and also time constraints on how long I could be out with him. What worked for us was to appeal to his reason and make deals. Before I allowed him (and other Afghan companions) off the leash in safe park grounds, I told them how long we had for the outing and when they needed to come back. I let them know my schedule and appointments and why they had to be back at a particular time. I also told them that if they did not come back in that time, they would be confined to the leash on the next day's outing. Most of the time, they kept to our set limits. They would stretch the time when I didn't have any set appointment to keep, as they knew it wasn't really serious. I was lax about it, too, and knew how important it was for them to have good exercise and exploration for their physical and emotional health. Though I took chances I may not ever take again, and we were definitely protected by our guardian angels, it worked for us.

Obedience training is beneficial when it is done with optimum communication and understanding of the dog. But there is a price that you pay when you use force and pain to demand obedience. I met a person who shook his young male Afghan by the neck and threw him on the ground on his back, supposedly imitating wolf pack discipline, a method that is used in a popular system of obedience training.

No alpha (leader) wolf throws another on the ground in submission; they agree to submit because of the respect they have for the leader, enforced by telepathic communication and body language that is mainly nonviolent. Yes, the Afghan was more obedient, out of fear and pain, but he withdrew into his own world and from then on refused to deeply share his inner self with his person. The dog got the terms of the relationship from the person and gave him the superficial obedience the person wanted, but he withheld sharing his deepest self after that.

I've been told by some breeders and trainers that some breeds or individuals need to be beaten or they will not respect you and won't listen. Others recommend hanging dogs by their collars, until they choke or pass out, to instill obedience. Dogs, like other animals, get your expectations and feelings and learn the game you play. If they think that they don't have to listen unless you use a certain level of force, then they don't. Yes, some breeds require some physical strength to handle, but the more you use harsh methods with them, the more they use their brute strength to handle you, instead of developing a reasoning relationship.

Different combinations of people and dogs do well together, and many kinds of relationships are possible. I find that if you can calm animals' fears and negative expectations and appeal to their intelligence, you have, in the long run, a saner and more peaceful, enjoyable, and expansive relationship. Trying to imitate alpha dog behavior and becoming a canine leader of the pack can set up an expectation in the dogs that you are like them, instead of a separate species with different behavior and viewpoints. It seems strange to me that humans would try to set themselves up as "top dog" instead of relating as a fellow, intelligent being of the human species and showing dogs what we need from them in their role as domestic animal helpers. We can honor their needs and understanding, as well as our own, if we recognize their different perceptions and realities and work things out together.

I have met dogs who, through breeding or misunderstanding, demand physical force from humans or they don't pay attention.

There are gentle ways to handle those who think they must be dealt with harshly: through counseling, gentle touch therapy and training (such as the TTEAM method developed by Linda Telling-ton Jones), and good communication methods. There is a small percentage of dogs who find it nearly impossible or undesirable to change from their aggressive habits, even when given numer-ous opportunities to learn other ways, but they are the exception.

I was staying for a few nights in the home of a woman who was sponsoring a lecture and workshop given by me. When I walked in the door, their two-year-old, 100+-pound Rottweiler dog, Max, greeted me by slamming his head between my legs (which he could barely get under because of his height) and blasting me against the wall. The woman apologetically, but laughingly, said he was just a puppy and he often did that to people. My back was now out of alignment, and I didn't see the humor of the "puppy's" behavior. When I sat down, he proceeded to chew on my wrist and hand, something else the "puppy" always did, she explained. She got a tug toy to distract him, but he seemed to prefer human arms.

Then I met the man of the house, an engineer and retired army officer. He shouted commands anytime the dog misbe-haved, and got temporary compliance some of the time. Mostly, he stuck chew and tug toys in his Rottweiler's mouth. I received the dog's thoughts about the game that he was playing. Max knew he wasn't really required to behave unless shouted at with deaf-ening decibels.

When Max continued to bother me, I told him that I knew he was intelligent and could understand me, and that I wasn't going to shout at him. I would ignore and avoid him unless he would listen to my needs and not shove me around. When I went to bed, I closed my door and told him that when he was willing to demonstrate his intelligence and respect my wishes, I would let him in.

After two days of coming and going at the house, with Max still acting unruly, especially when the husband was around, I woke up to find Max quietly lying outside my bedroom door, waiting for me. He let me know with his thoughts and demeanor that he was willing to listen now and act like the intelligent being I knew he was. I let him in and he calmly sat down, without pushing or mouthing. We had a great conversation about his role in life, and I gave him a gentle massage. After that, he behaved calmly and respectfully as I moved around the house. I felt we had made a real connection, and I hoped his life would be better, now that someone understood and brought out some of his depth, even though the man of the house was not receptive to telepathic communication.

I will never forget another Rottweiler named Jake, because he made me laugh so much. His person, Lucy, called me to find out what was going on with him in his advanced obedience training. Jake was fine at home practice and did every action perfectly, so she knew he understood and could do all the steps. When he got to the show ring, he would do goofy things, like throw the "dumb-bell" up in the air instead of bringing it back to her, or on the "long down," he would get up, turn around, bow and wag his tail in the air instead of quietly waiting for her signal. He was attracting quite a following of people who would wait to see what funny thing he would do next, and his person was feeling frustrated.

When I talked with Jake, he communicated to me that his person had told him that as soon as he did everything perfectly and got his title, he wouldn't have to go to shows anymore. He felt his purpose in life was to be a clown, to make people laugh and enjoy themselves, and he loved all the attention people gave him and the positive effects he created in them. He never wanted to stop going to those shows! Lucy confirmed that she, indeed, had promised that he wouldn't have to go to shows anymore. She thought Jake was getting bored with showing, and she just wanted him to get his title and award, then he could stay home.

Other dogs I have communicated with have been tired of shows and wanted to stay home and be a companion instead of a show dog. Some were bored from doing the same thing repetitively, and often had their titles already. Others felt showing was too stressful for them. Some enjoyed it for awhile, but then found it had become a serious competition between people rather than an interesting or challenging task for them, or mutual pleasure for canine and human.

Jake was different. He loved when people gathered around and laughed. He knew how to lighten the tension and help everyone have a good time. When Lucy heard Jake's viewpoint, she was surprised and relieved. We worked out a solution that pleased them both. I recommended that Lucy take Jake around to visit all the people before his time to show, so he could give them his warmth and good humor, as he loved to do. I asked him to run through the motions perfectly in the show ring, at least sometimes. Then people could see how capable he was, and his person could feel proud of him and receive the obedience title, which he was not concerned about, but which mattered to her. Lucy related to me weeks later that Jake loved going around before and after his show time to see everyone, and he easily got his title. She promised to take him to shows for as long as he wanted.

Helene Jaillet had attended a basic "how to communicate with animals" workshop. She then enrolled in a puppy obedience class at the Humane Society with her six-month-old Maltese dog, Mimi. They had missed one class, had hardly done any practicing, and so Helene did not expect to be able to do the "sit-stay" command very well that night, if at all. She tried to communicate with Mimi to ask that she *please* cooperate and do it, because Helene knew she could. Helene got the distinct feeling that Mimi was telling her that she found the whole thing very humiliating and didn't want to be doing any of this in the first place. Helene told her, "Well, it's going to look a lot more humiliating if we're the only ones who can't get it right! Everyone thinks you're the cutest puppy; you don't want them to think you're stupid." Helene also explained that everyone, including human children, go to school to learn certain behavior patterns. Again, Helene got a "feeling" that Mimi said she would think about it.

That night, when they went to class, everyone lined up and was told to give the "sit-stay" command while the instructor went around to all the puppies, bouncing a ball in front of their noses to see if they would remain still. At the end of the line, Helene doubted that Mimi would even sit long enough for the instructor to reach them. As Helene was looking at Mimi and silently begging her to please sit there, Mimi was laughing! Mimi looked at the other dogs who were not sitting still and being told "no!" by their distressed owners and then gaily looked straight back at Helene. The dog conveyed that this was a game, and they were going to win. Helene couldn't believe it, and silently promised Mimi the very best treat once they got home. Mimi thought it was really funny that they had this secret. The instructor came around and bounced the ball in front of Mimi; she just looked at her, as if to say, "That's nice," and then looked back at Helene again, amused at the whole thing. Helene shared Mimi's feelings and was having a hard time not laughing out loud.

The exercise was completed, and they were supposed to repeat it twice more. The second time, Mimi sat still almost to the very end. But the third time, she categorically decided that enough was enough, and this game had gotten boring. At that point, Helene really didn't care whether Mimi sat or didn't sit, since for her the sublime experience had been their communication.

This is not intended to be the ultimate advice on obedience training. Each dog will need and respond to different treatment. I do see the need for properly trained animals and humans for a functioning society! Using telepathic communication can help make obedience training a more intelligent, effective, and fun affair among people and their animal companions.

THE CAT WHO KNEW TOO MUCH

I have often been called upon to help with cats who pee or spray outside their litter box. Dixon was a three-year-old neutered male tabby, who, when his people called me, had been spraying around the house for a few months. The people were at their wits' end, as the furniture and carpets were being devastated. They were even considering exterminating Dixon if the problem could not be solved.

Communicating at a distance, Dixon showed me images and explained to me that there was a strange, wild dog coming to the sliding glass doors when his people were away. Dixon sprayed in the house as a signal that this was his and his family's territory. It also relieved the tension and fear he felt upon seeing this predator.

His people confirmed that the neighbors had seen coyotes in their yard. Dixon showed me that the family dogs lived in a kennel attached to the house. Rather than barking to chase the coyote away, they seemed to be in canine collusion with him, just watching as the coyote stared into the house. Dixon was the only one guarding. He had tried to alert his people to the danger, but they weren't listening, so he needed to spray to get their attention.

Well, it certainly did get their attention. Fortunately, they managed to understand his viewpoint before they decided to get rid of him. I suggested that they acknowledge Dixon's good intentions and his help in guarding home and family, and that they patrol for coyotes before they left home in the morning and when they came home. I checked with Dixon to see if this would help, and he was greatly relieved.

The people went around the house daily, assuring Dixon that there were no coyotes, and Dixon, now assured, stopped spraying in the house.

DECLAWING—
A CAT'S NIGHTMARE

Jackie called about her cat, Muffin, who was biting and scratching her people. Muffin had been affectionate and playful until after they got her simultaneously spayed and declawed. When I got in touch with Muffin, she had been severely traumatized. She experienced pain in her belly, severe pain in her toes, and hurtful anger at the perceived cruelty of her humans toward her. She didn't understand the reason for either of the operations, felt extremely vulnerable and frustrated, and responded by attacking her people.

I counseled Muffin and had her go through the incident of being spayed and declawed, to help release the trauma. It had been an excruciating ordeal for her. Her people had not explained what was going to happen. They did not realize that declawing is not a necessary operation and is accompanied by severe, often long-term, physical and emotional pain. Usually spaying is relatively untraumatic, and a cat heals from it without bad side effects, and with obvious positive benefits. The pain of declawing or having the first joints in her feet removed caused her to hold residual pain in her belly.

I explained to Muffin's people that, contrary to what some veterinarians tell you, the cats I have communicated with claim that declawing is a painful and emotionally harmful affair. It leaves the cat feeling vulnerable, since the front claws are a cat's first lines of defense. Often a cat who is declawed will begin to bite people, even in the face. When cats with claws intact scratch a tree or scratching post, they hook in their claws and stretch and align their whole spines, releasing locked up energy and increasing circulation throughout the body, thus helping to ensure good health. It is impossible for a cat to do this well without front claws. The toes often feel sore for months, even years, from the physical and psychological trauma. Many cats who are declawed go outside the litter box, especially to defecate. It hurts their sensitized paws to scratch the litter, and cats normally scratch to cover up their feces. Out of discomfort and protest, some declawed cats will urinate elsewhere.

It is not hard to train cats to use scratching posts if they are available near where the cat naps. Cats normally like to scratch after getting up, and they prefer textures that they can really hook their claws into, like the bark of trees, sisal rope, or the backside of carpeting, rather than the fluffy carpeting that is commonly sold for cat scratching posts. It helps to have smooth-textured furniture, instead of the nubby surfaces that cats find hard to resist scratching. Even where there is irresistibly textured furniture, with gentle persistence and well-placed and textured scratching posts, you can get most cats to enjoy scratching their posts, leaving the furniture alone. My four cats often scratch on the trees outside. Still, I have four cat scratching posts of different sizes and textures strategically placed for their convenience, so they have no excuse to scratch the furniture or carpets. They enjoy their choices, and I enjoy seeing them stretch and scratch to their hearts' content.

Imagine if you got your first finger joints cut off because you did things with your fingers that someone didn't like. What suffering and inhibited movement you would have! It is just as cruel with cats. You can communicate with them, and they can learn appropriate places to scratch. There are rare cases where cats would be killed if they weren't declawed. However, mutilation of animals' bodies (declawing, docking tails and ears) for human convenience or cosmetic consideration is cruel, and many animals who undergo such operations suffer behavioral, psychological, or physical disorders as a result.

The long-distance counseling and healing with Muffin was successful. She released her pain and emotional frustration, and returned to peaceful, loving coexistence with her people. To aid the healing of feline and humans, her people gave her gentle massages and special playtimes, and most of all, they understood her position.

THE FERAL CAT LISTENED

Dave looked after a number of feral cats in his area, as well as adopting some to be indoor cats. He fed the wild ones outdoors and trapped them for spaying and neutering to prevent overpopulation and territorial fighting. He called me because he was very concerned about one young female cat, pregnant with her second litter of kittens, whom he had tried to trap repeatedly and unsuccessfully. She refused to enter the baited cage.

When I communicated with her long-distance, she immediately sent a wave of terror about the trap. To her, it equaled death. Being caught by humans was the worst torture she could imagine. I listened and acknowledged her fear, which helped her to be receptive to what I had to say. I explained what Dave was doing with the trap: that she would be spayed so that she wouldn't have to have babies anymore, which could exhaust her and cause her to die prematurely. I explained that she would be taken to a hospital for the operation, but that she would be released after recovery. It would hurt only for a short time, and then she would be free and not have to be pregnant again. She was terrified that she might be kept "prisoner" in the house. I ensured that Dave guaranteed she would be released and not kept indoors against her will.

The cat did not give me a definite answer as to whether she would cooperate, so I just left it to her to make her decision. Dave called the next day, astonished. He said, "I don't know what you did to that cat, but she walked right into the trap that evening." He got her spayed and kept his promise to release her.

When we moved into our home in 1988, a feral tomcat who roamed the area terrorized our cats, physically hurting Heyoka and Sherman, and emotionally stressing everyone. I communicated with him that his actions were not okay. I did not want to hurt him, but I did not want him harming our cats either. Our neighbors had trapped and killed a feral cat who was ravaging the birds that came to their feeder and consuming wildlife on national parkland nearby, and I warned him the same could happen to him. I felt him listening.

His visits became less frequent, but after he attacked Heyoka again, I threatened him with trapping. I even got a Havahart trap from the Humane Society to show him I meant business. I told him I didn't really want to use it, besides thinking I'd probably end up with a skunk or raccoon. He never bothered us again, and I only saw him once, outside our fence, grooming himself in the sun.

HORSES RELEASE THEIR PAIN

After communicating with thousands of horses, it is clear to me that a lot of problems that humans and horses have in their relationships with each other stem from humans' misunderstanding of what horses are really feeling and thinking. People often complain that their horses are stubborn or suddenly resistant or ornery. They usually explain how they, or their trainer, have forced the horse to carry on, despite the animal's unruliness. While this temporarily "worked"—that is, their horse got through the lesson somehow—now the horse is biting, rearing, or bucking when they ride, or even when people approach.

Horses often tell me of how they hurt, that they just can't bear the pain anymore. The pain can come from injuries, new or flared up because of physical pressure or emotional stress, or be aggravated by improper riding habits, awkward saddles, or some other physical imbalance. People are not usually trained to notice the first signs of a horse's discomfort, or equine attempts to communicate that something is wrong. Imagine how you would feel if you had an aching head, neck, or back, and someone insisted on pushing you around. Would you feel ornery, stubborn, fearful, or resistant? You bet!

After getting the horse to describe the location and nature of the pain, tightness, or imbalance that is causing misbehavior, we have usually found a gentle and sensible method to handle it. It may require a new saddle or pad, balanced shoeing, chiropractic alignment, acupuncture sessions, changes in diet, or some other veterinary assistance or bodywork, emotional counseling of horse and human, more balanced riding by the person, rest, or a combination of these. It usually doesn't just go away by carrying on riding as usual.

Laura explained that her ten-year-old Thoroughbred dressage horse, Gator, had been refusing to "come on the bit" and stride forward, though sometimes he would do just fine. Gator pictured that he had severe neck tension and some pain in the forehead. I asked him about dressage and the problem his person related, and he clearly relayed that he worried about doing well. When he got nervous about understanding what was asked of him or whether he was doing it just right, he would tighten his jaw and compress his neck, which constricted his shoulder movement; therefore, he could not move out freely.

Although Gator had prior misalignments in the neck, corrected by acupuncture, it was not the cause of this problem. His self-induced, emotionally stressful state caused him to clamp up and lose his connection with his whole body. However, when he was relaxed, he was able to stride forward gracefully. Once he compressed his jaw and neck, his nervousness would increase, and he was no longer able to think clearly and stay in touch with his person. He would become distracted and even more distressed, as he wanted to do everything well, and was trying too hard.

To disengage this cycle, I recommended that Laura do some touch-massage on his body, particularly the forehead, jaw, and lower neck, to help Gator to relax. She should then talk to him about the agenda for the day, explaining just what she'd like him to do, in a clear and relaxed way. Then, when she was riding, she should watch for his habit of clamping his jaw and neck. By reminding him to ease up and stretch his neck out, explaining and picturing to him what she wanted him to do, and gently helping him to round his neck and engage again, she would help him to replace the old habit with the new. I advised her to do a touch session after riding, relaxing her horse again, and praising him for all the right things he did, to boost his confidence in himself.

Gator showed immediate and steady improvement after an acupuncture session, which eased the tension in his neck and improved his overall balance; the follow-up actions I had recommended helped him to release the emotional stress and physical habits.

A somewhat similar case involved a horse named Maxwell. His people had a problem with his riding stiffly and being resistant to turning, particularly to the left. He told me that his neck and back hurt from an old injury that occurred in a trailer, and his training was hard on him and made him respond to riding by tensing his muscles. I worked gently with his body, helping him to notice where he was holding tension and pain. As I worked with him, I asked him to release where he was holding, and he visibly relaxed. He showed me, with mental images, how he tensed his body while he was being ridden, and that he had certain habits that made riding uncomfortable. I explained to his people to gently touch him before they rode and to remind him to release his habitual tensing while they were riding him, so he could feel more relaxed and not create soreness and pain for himself.

Besides noting Maxwell's evident acceptance of my directions as I worked on him, the people were delighted with how he responded to their offering advice to him as they rode. When he was reminded to release his neck or back, he would noticeably relax and change his old habits, and riding became smoother and more pleasurable. In a few weeks, after having been stiff and tense for years, Maxwell looked like a new horse. The direct communication enlisting his help and understanding enhanced the effectiveness of the bodywork.

Dominic, a large Thoroughbred horse, was acting up under saddle. He explained that the middle of his back was sore. I scanned over and lightly touched his back, explaining to him and his person where the vertebrae were compressed, causing him pain. The horse listened and rounded his back up, whereupon we heard the vertebrae go *pop pop pop*. He also indicated to me that he wanted to roll and further relax and release his spine. He felt he had been working too hard, tensing his spine when trying to perfectly execute the dressage movements. His person led him out to a good rolling area, where he thoroughly enjoyed himself. Later, when ridden, Dominic moved smoothly and comfortably.

I have often found that when you point out to animals what is causing the pain and visualize or tell them how they can help to release it, they do all or most of the work themselves, without the aid of elaborate adjustments or bodywork. When using gentle bodywork techniques, it helps to give them plenty of leeway to participate, and to explain everything you're doing along the way.

This enlists their cooperation, just as it does with humans, and the whole process of releasing and healing is made shorter and more pleasant. Using forceful or imposed techniques without enlisting the animal's understanding and cooperation may cause resistance, further pain, physical constriction, or a temporary release, which bounces back in a short time to the former tense state.

Jim Dietz told me that after learning to communicate with animals at a basic workshop, his animals at home looked at him very differently, and he felt a transformed relationship with them. One day, a wild horse he had adopted was thrashing and biting at her side with obvious pain from colic. He slipped her halter on, which the horse would not normally let him do, and walked her around. Her condition did not improve. He called the vet to come, which would take an hour.

The horse was unable to eat and kept crashing to the ground, rolling and biting at her side; he feared that he might lose her. He then put his arms around her, told her how special she was to him, and that he loved her with all his heart and really wanted her to stay. In a short time, the horse got up, began to eat and pass gas and manure, and acted like nothing ever happened. He canceled the vet appointment.

THE CANARY WOULDN'T SING

Our canary, Frodo, sang beautifully, especially in the morning or whenever my husband would play on the guitar or lute a piece of music that Frodo particularly appreciated. He lived in a large cage in the living room with Sultan, a strawberry finch, with whom he had become a very good buddy after Sultan's mate died. In early summer 1992, Frodo stopped singing. I wasn't that concerned about it, as he was molting, and canaries often stop singing while their bodies are putting all their energy into making a new set of feathers. Many months went by and Frodo still did not sing, whereas in previous years he had resumed his singing within a few months after molting was completed. I queried him about it.

He felt that there was something wrong with his throat, but that it would heal and he would sing again. I was surprised, as he always looked fit and active. After more weeks of no singing, I decided to explore the matter further with Frodo. Frodo felt there was still something wrong with his throat, which prevented him from singing. I received images of scar tissue in the throat. This puzzled me, as Frodo had never shown any signs of illness.

I asked if there could be any other reason for his not singing. He felt embarrassed as he answered. When Frodo used to sing joyfully and frequently, he would stop Sultan from singing. If the little strawberry finch started on his lovely tune, Frodo would chase him from his perch. Sultan could only sing uninterrupted while Frodo was busy eating. Most of the time, they were buddies and slept and ate together happily. There was just the issue of singing. Frodo realized, as we communicated about it, that he stopped himself from singing so that he would allow Sultan to expand and sing whenever he wanted to. The consequence was that his throat actually felt physically blocked. We told him we'd love to hear him sing again, and he could allow Sultan to sing in turn, too.

The next morning, Frodo began to trill quietly for the first time in months, though not with his old exuberance. We thanked and encouraged him. Then he stopped, and after a few days, I checked with him again. He said he felt that if he sang fully, his feeling of dominance and territoriality would return, and he would be impelled to stop Sultan again. He just didn't want to do that.

I could see that this was a process for Frodo—to learn how to express himself fully without feeling the need to suppress his buddy, Sultan. I felt he could do it, so we encouraged Frodo to sing in a new way. We suggested that if he felt the feelings of dominance toward his fellow bird friend, he could fly around the cage and let the feelings fly out without directing them at Sultan. He could appreciatively listen to Sultan sing, and learn to take turns. He said he'd try.

The next morning he again sang, tentatively and quietly. Sultan also changed his behavior. From being very submissive and careful toward Frodo, he sang out more and called in different ways. They even began to sing together—something we had never heard before.

AN OLD BIRD LEARNS
NEW TRICKS

Pirouette, my first cockatiel companion, was given to me when he was two and a half years old. He was not tamed to come on a hand or even a perch, and basically stayed in his cage. He whistled a basic cockatiel chirp and wolf whistle and didn't talk. My favorite thing to say to him in the beginning was "You're terrific, Pirouette." Within a few weeks he was saying, "You're terrific," over and over. He had already mastered the new name he gave himself, Pirouette.

I whistled "Yankee Doodle" and "The Star Spangled Banner" to him, and in a few weeks, he had mastered those. I told him that instead of continuing to whistle songs for him to learn, he could learn his own from the radio. We played a classical music station for him a few hours daily, and in a short time, we were guessing from which pieces he was singing, as he gaily strung musical phrases together. After a few months, he was improvising his own classical and jazz compositions, with an occasional "Yankee Doo-dle" or "Star Spangled Banner" thrown in.

Behavior books say that birds are best tamed and trained when they are babies. Pirouette was an adult, and definitely did not like human fingers near him. He told me he did not want to be tamed to a perch or hand; he felt it was undignified. I honored his wishes, but he did love faces to be close to him, and I often kissed, talked, whistled, and sang to him through the bars of his cage. Later, when I got a mate for him, and they were breeding, his behavior was challenging. When he did fly around with his mate, Opal, he could not be easily caught, and ferociously bit me if I got my hands near him. He was still adamant about not being tamed. After Opal found a new home and Pirouette's breeding days ended, he happily returned to his cage.

At eight years old, after living most of his life in roomy cages, he said that he wanted to come out, sit on the table, and eat breakfast with us. I told him, in order to do that, he'd have to learn to sit on a perch and hand without fussing or biting, or it wouldn't be safe to have him flying around the house. I was amazed when he agreed to learn to do this, at his age, after being adamant all these years.

So, I rolled his cage into the bathroom for training sessions. In two days with a twenty-minute session each day, he was peacefully and easily going on a perch and my arm and finger. Pirouette then enjoyed eating our breakfast cereal with us and flying around the house. After a few weeks of that, he said, "That's enough. That was fun, but now I don't want to do that anymore." He then refused to get on perches and hands again. Four years later, he decided to be "tame" again and returned to flying sessions and walks around the table, occasionally taking a bite of our food.

Many people have the conception that animals don't think much, that they certainly don't think creatively or change their minds consciously. Pirouette, and many others, show the limitations of that idea.

DANCING WITH A LLAMA

I first met llamas in 1976, when I was visiting the Los Angeles Zoo. Their enclosure was on a hill at the top of the zoo, rarely visited by other humans because of the long climb. I stood on the walkway looking up at three llamas in the far corner of their pasture near their feeding shed. I asked if they would come out, so I could see them better and visit with them. I got a feeling of disdain, almost disgust, in return. *They* come down for *me*—a lowly human?

So, I offered to sing for them. As I sang, it perked their inter-est, and they looked, but they wouldn't come closer. I said, "All right, I'll dance for you." I proceeded to dance on the broad side-walk, and the lead llama came running down to get close to me. The others came closer too, but she warned them back, saying, "This is for me alone."

She accompanied me in my dance, back and forth along the fence. I felt her enjoyment and the oneness of understanding we had of grace in movement. We were partners in our aesthetic appreciation. The two other llamas were entranced and tried to join in, but they obeyed the leader's imperious command. We carried on in song and dance for about fifteen minutes, until the zoo bell sounded that it was time for closing.

I explained to my llama dance partner that I had to go. She told me that I was to continue. I did for awhile, until the bell warned again. She told me, "You will come back," in her com-manding way. I said that I would, and I looked back at her as I reluctantly walked away. She watched after me for awhile, then turned back up her hill.

THE CHICKEN GUARDIANS

A dream come true—our own two llama companions, Regalo and Raindance, arrived December 6, 1991. One of the benefits of their presence was their guardian quality. Before they arrived, each year we would lose a few chickens to foxes and weasels who managed to squeeze through the chicken enclosure by noticing wire corroding or loosening before we saw it. Our dogs always heard and chased raccoons away from the chicken run, but the smaller predators were too silent and swift.

The llamas' fenced area surrounded the chicken run, and I let the llamas know that guarding the chickens from predators was one of their jobs. With llamas' natural alertness, curiosity, and guarding ability, I felt that now the chickens would always be safe from attack.

In August 1992, when I was taking some friends around the llama run, I saw raccoon scat on the ground near the end of the chicken run farthest away from the llama shelter. I mentioned to the visitors that I was surprised, for I hadn't noticed raccoons around since the llamas had taken the job of official chicken guardians. I was concerned and mentioned to my visitors that I hoped the llamas would keep on alert for predators. I never mentioned it directly to Regalo and Raindance.

That night, I couldn't see the llamas resting in their usual spots near or in their shed, so I went looking for them. Both of them were lying down not far from the raccoon scat, facing the chicken run. I had never seen them sleep there before. They were surprised when I went looking for them; both assumed that I wanted them to guard there. They have since taken up their stations there at night when they perceive it necessary.

THE RATTLESNAKE THAT DIDN'T STRIKE

My only knowledge of rattlesnakes came secondhand, from Western movies where the cowboy shot, or had his horse trample, the dangerous creatures before they struck. My first encounter with a rattlesnake in 1982 showed me a whole different aspect of their nature.

We were hiking the hilly trails of Griffith Park in Los Angeles with our dogs. Rana, our female Afghan, was running just ahead of us, when I heard the loud rattle. We got Pasha on the leash and quickly caught up to Rana, who was less than a year old. She was bouncing around and woofing at a large, coiled-up rattlesnake. The snake was ready to strike, and Rana, in her great excitement, did not heed my pleas to come or move away.

I knew that if I hurriedly grabbed for her, the snake might strike me. So, I calmly told the snake that we did not mean to harm him; Rana was just a puppy playing. I was going to reach for Rana and take her away from disturbing him, and we would walk in the other direction. I respectfully asked if he would uncoil and go the other way. I then grabbed Rana's collar and pulled her away. The snake stopped rattling, uncoiled, and traveled in the opposite direction.

HARMONY WITH THE YELLOW JACKETS

When we moved to our own home in 1988, I noticed wasps flying into a hole under a section of wooden fence. My knowledge of wasps was limited to their building nests under the eaves of houses, so I wondered what they were doing in the ground. I approached slowly and asked the busy wasps if I could peek into their opening to see what they were doing. I got an "okay," so

I knelt on the ground and peered into the hole. Wasps flew in and out, all around my face, as I gazed in fascination at their honeycomb-patterned nest. I thanked the wasps as I withdrew, and I got a definite answer of, "You're welcome, but now keep a distance from our home and leave us alone."

A few days later, a biologist wrote in our local paper about how nasty yellow jacket wasps were, that they attacked humans without provocation. My encounter with them had been totally different, and we worked side by side in the garden without any problem. I was never stung.

Each summer, the yellow jacket community made their nest in a different spot in the garden, and came and went without incident. In 1992, they chose a rotting stump about three feet from my garden work area, near the outdoor sink and hose. One day, as I was watering the garden, I didn't notice the hose sliding back and forth across their entry hole. An angry sentry wasp let me know that they didn't like that. It was my first wasp sting.

I experienced firsthand their warrior nature in defense of their home, and I reacted in hurt and anger. Then I could identify more with what the biologist had written. The next morning I did an uncharacteristic act of retaliation: I stuffed their hole with debris and soil. As I walked around the garden, a warrior wasp came right for me. I brushed him off before he stung, and I apologized, embarrassed at my "eye for an eye" reflex. I experienced the emotions that cause wars and saw the futility of it. I explained my position to the wasps and respectfully asked for a truce. I would respect their home, but they had to respect my position as keeper of the garden, who helped the flowers grow that they so enjoyed.

We did fine after that. I had to be very conscious of them and emanate peace and respect whenever I went by their domicile. It was difficult to haul the hose around the garden without sliding it past their home. They would swarm when that happened, and I would bless them with peace and respect and make my presence scarce until they calmed down. My husband, Michel, went by their home one day after I had used the hose and they hadn't yet fully calmed down, and one stung him. He was angry and wanted to get rid of them. I felt his reaction and theirs, and the need for a truce with every human who passed. Living in peace with these easily aroused neighbors required a high degree of consciousness and calmness.

We lived for six months with them, and I figured winter rain and cold would end their stay with us. It was December, near freezing, and still they persisted. I had asked them to leave, and I got the answer that they were slowly departing, but still they swarmed if disturbed by people's movements. We always had to warn people of their presence, and several people advised us of ways to kill them, wondering why we hadn't done it already. We would explain our policy of coexistence.

My tolerance limit was reached when my rabbit, Ellyetta, on a jaunt around the yard, went near their nest, and they went after her. One stung her and several more tried to, but I brushed them away as I rushed her to safety in her bunny cottage. To prevent an allergic reaction, I gave her a homeopathic remedy for stings. She was okay, but my tolerance for the wasps was fractured. We were supposed to be living in harmony, but the balance was lopsided. I sent them peace and respect and they, like tyrants, sent out demands, irritability, and pain.

I told them I had enough of their presence, and I was planning to help them go. So that night I covered their stump entrance thickly with diatomaceous earth, which has a dehydrating effect on insect bodies, but is harmless to the rest of the environment and is a soil nutrient. They still came out rather undeterred, but after days of continued applications, a cold spell, and piling their entrance with rocks, they weakened and died. It was a hard decision on my part, but I had to face the fact that peaceful communication was not the whole solution in this situation.

THE MYSTERY OF THE "BUGGLES"

Most of my life, I've practiced harmonious coexistence with insects, having great success with peacefully contacting the oversoul of ant or cockroach colonies whose members inhabited my apartments. With cleaning up any food attractions, proper respect, some bargaining, and offerings being given to them, they have willingly left my living space.

When a sudden and profuse invasion of tiny insects appeared in our cupboards in 1990, I was stymied when they did not respond to the usual quiet connection, communication, and parlaying that had worked before. In fact, I found I could receive little meaningful communication from them at all. I wondered if they were some alien or mutated species, suddenly materializing, because they seemed especially attracted to plastic bags and containers, even when the plastic had never contained any trace of food. No one I knew could identify what they were, so I affectionately called them the "buggles."

It is my policy not to use poisons, and I did not use any other physical deterrents, other than sealing up all my food in containers. The buggles continued to multiply. With no communication arriving from them to bring another solution, I reluctantly ended up wiping their vast numbers off the floor and counters and flushing them down the sink. This went on for weeks, and my actions and lack of success in communication embarrassed me.

Then I warned the group that I would have to put out diatomaceous earth in the cupboards, which would dehydrate their bodies if they did not leave. After issuing that ultimatum, while taking an afternoon nap, I got an image of an entity that I knew was the "leader" or oversoul of the buggles. I asked the leader why the buggles had come to our house, and it said that they were attracted by the wonderful energy here, that they wanted to be a part of our family and help in interspecies communication.

I acknowledged and honored the purity of that message, but I then made it clear that from my human viewpoint, having millions of buggle bodies crawling over my kitchen was undesirable. Couldn't they just be present and contribute in spirit? The leader saw my point and told me that the buggles would handle the situation by crawling into the containers of diatomaceous earth that I put in the corners of the cupboards. In the weeks that followed, hordes of buggles marched into the containers and dried up, and their physical population gradually disappeared from my house. I still feel their loving spiritual presence adding to the welcoming energy and harmony here.

THE WHALES RETURN

I've always had a special affinity for whales. They are ancient guardians, the wise ones of the sea. Kinship with them runs deep and long for me. I believe that without their presence on the Earth, ecological balance and harmony would be destroyed, and humankind would be spiritually lost and soon perish.

In 1979, a person wrote me a letter asking if I could do something about the decimation of the whales by humans. I communicated with my whale brothers and sisters, and I was told by the chief/oversoul of the largest whales that their time had come to leave the Earth. They were the guardians and teachers of wisdom for humanity and the rest of the Earth. They felt that reaching humans was beyond hope now, since humans continued to decimate the whales and the rest of the Earth's animal population. I conveyed that I felt there was hope, that so many people were becoming aware of their spiritual nature and seeking wisdom from the natural world again. Could they please stay?

The whales and I conversed, communed, and prayed together for awhile. I was giving solo dance performances at the time and promised to dedicate dances to the whales and their return to keep the brother/sisterhood of whales and humans intact. When I danced in the following months and years, I could feel their connection and decision to regroup, repopulate, and return. I'm sure that the conscientious efforts of many others paralleled my dances and prayers, and I felt that these gestures from all of us were important in reestablishing the guardianship of the whales, so necessary for our harmonious existence.

I could not be on the Earth if the animals and plants were gone. I wouldn't live in artificial environments, with a barren Earth environment, just to stay physically alive. My very being is linked with all other beings; my work with humans would not be possible without the support and power of the animals and other species.

The whales honor me with their presence during whale watching expeditions and migrations. People have commented that even when they haven't seen whales in weeks, when I am there, the whales appear. I may feel more at one with whales than any other species on the Earth. This is very hard to say, for I feel that link with every species I encounter! However, when I think about the whales, I feel a resonance in my heart, and throughout the breadth and depth of the universe. They understand the plight of humans and have renewed their pledge to help.

Oh beautiful beings in giant forms
That grace the ocean wide
Your message to creatures of the land
You've brought on every tide

You've sailed along right at our side.
Human ignorance has torn at your massive bones
You've caused us no harm
Even your anger is a lesson.

Do not leave us
Help us to complete your mission of wisdom
In gratefulness I shed my tears

Be with us more, giant companions
Till this Earth glows from ocean to ocean
In renewed spirit, petty games abandoned.

I pledge my forward thrust
In parallel united motion
Water-flow spirits create the waves
Needed to replenish the barren lands.

Stay with us, noble ones
Show me how to add strength to my mission
Thank you ever for yours, oh brothers and sisters
Peace over the waves and through
To the blue-green dawn.

In about 1985, a gray whale called Humphrey made the news worldwide, when he crossed under the Golden Gate Bridge, through San Francisco Bay, and up the Sacramento River to his seeming doom in the shallows. People tried various methods to get this apparently lost or disoriented whale to turn around, back to the open sea.

When I communicated with Humphrey, he showed me that he was a special emissary who had been chosen by his group of whales to expand the consciousness of humans. He was aware that he could die in his mission, but he would not turn around until enough humans were moved to become aware of and change what they were doing to the whales, the oceans, and all life on Earth. For weeks, the media proclaimed his travail and unsuccessful human efforts to save him. When a certain level of contact and awareness had been reached, Humphrey let people help him to return. I could feel the joy in the whale, ocean, and world community when he accomplished his mission.

In 1991, Dawn Hayman communicated with three whales who were trapped beneath ice off the coast of Alaska, unable to surface:

> The media covered the story on a daily basis as men worked desperately to cut holes in the ice, inviting the whales to surface and breathe. But the whales kept moving away from them. My partner, Bonnie, asked me to speak to the whales and tell them that if they went to the holes in the ice, they would be helped. I contacted the whales and was rather surprised at what I heard. "We are not here to be saved," they began. "We three have been chosen to teach humans a very important lesson. We are not trapped here unwillingly." I explained to them that they would die if they kept going further into the ice. They replied, "We will have to die to teach our lesson. We are not sad; we are honored to be the ones chosen for the task."
>
> I didn't understand, but I accepted their words. Each morning before hearing the news, Bonnie would ask me to contact the whales. One morning they told me that one of them had died and that the other two were moving on, further into the ice. When I asked them what lesson humankind was supposed to learn from this, they only said that we would find out.

The news that afternoon confirmed what I learned from the whales. One whale had died, and the others were moving further from the air holes. Bonnie and I were sad knowing the whales would die, wondering about the lesson they meant to die to teach us.

The following morning, Bonnie once again asked me to contact the whales. When I did, I got a surprise. "We are going to live!" began the overjoyed whale. "You humans not only got our message, but far surpassed what we thought you would do. Now we can teach the lesson better by living." I was filled with joy. They were so proud, so excited, and so honored by something we humans had done or understood. We wondered what it was. Then we turned on the news. The Russians were sending out an icebreaker. So were the Americans. They were to meet, and clear a channel for the whales to the sea. This operation would take time, but if the whales would use the air holes, they could make it. Late that morning, the whales turned back and began using the air holes. The icebreakers continued towards one another until they met, and the whales swam free to the sea.

Many months later, Bonnie and I realized the significance of my communication with the whales. Two icebreakers, from countries that had been bitter enemies for decades, and which had never cooperated with each other in such a humanitarian way, came together in that cold sea, and broke the ice to save life. Our teachers, the whales, knew this. Thank goodness we human beings got their message. The teachers no longer have to die to save us.

PROBLEM

PREVENTION

AND LIFE

ENHANCEMENT

ANIMALS AND CHILDREN are often treated as if they weren't concerned with what goes on in the family. As leaders of the household, adults often make decisions and changes that affect their animal companions or children without letting them know what's happening. Sometimes this causes long-term physical and mental suffering. Here's an example:

Tara was a very forlorn Irish setter, who had been presenting a slight fever and refusal to eat when her person called me for help. All Tara could tell me was that she felt sad. I asked her person if Tara had experienced a loss of someone or something before the change in behavior occurred. He mentioned that he had broken up with his girlfriend a few weeks ago.

Hearing this, Tara started talking to me about how she missed the girl so much. We communicated awhile, getting all of Tara's thoughts and feelings about the subject. It turned out that Tara thought that she was to blame for the breakup. She had been so happy with both of her human friends, until the time they closed the door and talked for many hours, leaving Tara confused as to what was going on. The next thing Tara knew, the girl was packing and leaving. Not knowing what went on between the two people, she went into grief and hopelessness, blaming herself and thinking she must have done something very bad for this to happen.

No one had explained the situation to Tara, not thinking how she would be affected by it or that she needed to know. Some people do the same with children. Thinking children wouldn't understand anyway, they fail to make clear what really is happening in events that concern them. The person or animal may feel responsible for the bad situation. They may experience anxiety, confusion, or despair over it.

Tara really brightened upon relating this and earlier instances of this type of misunderstanding. She returned to her normal enthusiasm when she found out what really happened, with the promise of seeing her person's ex-girlfriend again.

Not all animals are equally sensitive or needful of being carefully informed. Know your animal friend. Don't tell your animal companions (or children) that everything is okay when it isn't. They may feel shocked or confused when they find out the truth, or generate their own interpretation of what is going on.

Gently and honestly communicate the real situation in a way that can be understood, so they have a chance to absorb it. Being left in confusion can be hazardous to your animal friend's mental and physical health. An unexplained loss can result in illness or even injury from accidents brought on by emotional strain, which can throw animals out of phase with their surroundings. Be sure your animal friends understand. This can prevent a lot of distress.

A simple matter of letting your animal companions know how long you'll be gone from home and that you'll return can ease anxiety. Don't worry about what other people think when they hear you talking things over with your animal friends. It may even jog their preconceived notions about animal intelligence and help them to respect and understand animals more. Criticism should be tossed aside when your own and your animal friends' happiness is at stake.

PURPOSES

This section may help change your whole relationship with your animal companions. Here's how:

Ensure that each of your animal friends has, knows, and fulfills a purpose.

By doing this, you may avoid many behavior problems and thereby increase happiness and life expectancy. You will tend to respect and treat animals more as intelligent beings. They will feel happier and more responsible and responsive, because they are truly contributing or helping as members of the family.

Let me relate the case of a poodle named Zor. Zor's person couldn't understand and didn't know what to do about Zor's destructiveness when he left him in the yard to go to work for the day. Zor would bang on the back door and windows until he managed to break into the house. The person had not wanted to leave

Zor in the house while he was gone for fear he would pee on or chew something.

Zor was very intelligent and direct in his communication to me. He made it clear that he wanted to be close to his human friend, even when he went to work, by being inside the house where he could guard his person's belongings. It frustrated Zor so much to be left out in the yard. He feared someone might get into the house and tamper with his person's treasured stereo and photographic equipment.

The reason he had peed and chewed on things before was to mark his person's belongings, out of anxiety that someone would touch them while Zor was not around, since his person did not allow Zor to guard them directly. Not understanding Zor's behavior and thinking his dog could not understand what he said, he never explained to Zor exactly what was needed. The person also thought Zor would be happier all day in the fresh air and never clearly observed what the dog really wanted to do.

By communicating with both dog and person, we cleared up all the misunderstandings about each other's behavior, with smiles all around. (Dogs do smile, but not always with their mouths as humans do!) The person decided to let Zor stay in the house and guard all day. The results were a very cheerful, responsible dog and a more understanding, happy human.

The preceding story exemplifies why it's so important to establish your animal friend's purpose or position in the family. Here is a general approach:

First observe what your cat, horse, dog, turtle, or bird likes and is genetically suited to do, and what activity enhances your coexistence. For example, your Siamese cat likes to keep her area clean, your German shepherd likes to look after the kids, or your Chihuahua takes pride in patrolling your yard and barking when strangers approach.

Talk it over with your animal friends, and establish what purposes or jobs they can fulfill in relation to you and your environment. Be sure the functions are suited to the animal's physical capacities. Don't ask your turtle to answer the phone and take messages, even though she wants to communicate with your friends. Ask her instead to look after the apartment by radiating her brightness and warm presence there. Ask your Siamese to help keep the place clean and cheerful, your German shepherd to watch the kids when they play in the yard.

Don't punish animals when they don't seem to do exactly as you want. Be patient and clear up any disagreements or misunderstandings. Reestablish what is needed that the animals can reasonably deliver, in alignment with their natural physical and personal inclinations.

Other examples of jobs or purposes that many animals take up happily are: keeping you happy; cheering you up when you're down; entertaining the family with antics; creating warmth around the house so all feel welcome; adding beauty to the environment with their physical appearance, mannerisms, song, or purr; guarding property; creating a feeling of safety so that no negative influences can enter; getting you out to exercise; keeping you calm and soothing tensions; expanding your viewpoints about life; sharing or enhancing an activity you enjoy, such as running, swimming, Frisbee competition, or equestrian skills;

or even assisting you with your work or other activities spiritually at a distance.

After I gave a lecture, a man with five small dogs decided to take my advice. His dogs normally competed with each other for his attention and created chaos when he walked in the door. So now he communicated with each one separately, let them know their special task, and acknowledged them for doing well when they responded to him. To his surprise, his dogs settled down and were considerably easier to live with—and the whole family was happier.

Before I would leave the house, if I were not taking my male Afghan hound, Pasha, with me, I let him know where I was going, approximately how long I'd be gone, why I couldn't take him, and what I expected from him while I was gone, such as taking care of the house or looking after the cats. When I returned, I'd quickly inspect the area, thank Pasha for doing his job, and give him thanks or a hug of appreciation. Even though he wished he could have gone with me, this made any disappointment vanish, as he was contributing to our collective well-being and he could feel valuable and loved.

The departure does not have to be a long, drawn-out ritual when your animal friends are accustomed to your direct communication. Just a matter-of-fact, quick thought, and it's all understood. For years, I didn't need to go into great detail with Pasha when I was leaving, since he was well versed in what to expect and he did his job well.

Another example of how animals respond to having a worthwhile job to do was the case of Anna, a horse. She was being cared for by a lady who had not ridden her, as she had had a bad experience on another horse and was afraid to ride again.

Anna had the reputation of being stubborn and hard to ride. I saw as I talked to her that she was a very wise being who had been handled with lack of respect by the people who held this poor opinion of her. When I explained to Anna that her person was afraid of horses since her bad experience and needed help to regain confidence, Anna was very soft and understanding. The lady was overjoyed when later she rode Anna and had a great experience, which restored her confidence around horses.

Most beings respond to honesty and sincerity. Animals will normally sense your fears, anger, or other feelings anyway, so there's no use trying to cover them up. It's best to talk over how you feel and what you need in order to establish a basis for cooperation and understanding. With your communication basics properly applied, you will know if they are with you in spirit. Most will be.

I had a similar experience with a reputedly high-strung horse in one of my first times in the saddle. This was the riding instructor's mare, who normally responded only to her person, and we were going to have a lesson. I respected the horse's sensitivity and intelligence, and I told her that I was a novice and would appreciate gentle treatment.

While I was riding, the instructor was amazed when the horse obeyed my wishes to slow down over her own directions to speed up. Even though they had great rapport, the horse was empathetic with my needs because of the communication we had established. The horse was being kind to me and helping me have a good experience, and I truly appreciated it!

When an animal's job or purpose is firmly recognized, validated, and established, near miraculous cooperation and joy can appear with previously destructive, moody, or generally unhappy animals. Those animals that are already in happy harmony with you are productive members of their family or society who know, enjoy, and fulfill their purposes. We all appreciate being included and contributing to each other as best we can.

FREEDOM, CONTROL, AND OBEDIENCE

Are you confused regarding how much freedom you should give your animal companions? Does the subject of rules, control, or obedience send you spinning?

Some people insist that their animal companions be under their strict control, obeying them at all times. They punish animals who relax even slightly from their regimen. They are the masters, and their animals are the slaves. Both behave like robots in relationship to each other, the person constantly domineering and the animal always subservient.

In the other extreme, the human allows animal companions to do anything. There are no rules. If the animals want to walk all over dinner on the table or pee on the bed, they are pampered and catered to, no matter how inconvenient it is for others. The person has a propitiating or sickening, sympathetic attitude toward animals, who dominate the human's behavior toward them.

Between both extremes fall most of us with animals in the family. We all may wonder at times how strict we should be in handling our animal companions, what freedoms we should allow, and what the rules should be.

There is no rote answer to this issue, as a lot depends on individual preference and circumstances. There should be known, consistent, consensual freedoms and rules for the sanity and happiness of all involved. Animal companions need certain common-sense freedoms to fulfill their nature, like freedom to exercise and play and be a part of the family.

There have to be rules that establish the limits of acceptable and unacceptable behavior. These may vary according to lifestyle and needs, but if there are no definite rules, then there is unpredictability and confusion on how to function as a family member. Animals may then fill the void with patterns from their genetic backgrounds or with other actions you might not like that they have picked up from other animals (including humans). This may end up making them and the people around them very unhappy.

I've talked with a number of dogs who have become aggressive toward people, ferociously rushing and barking at them or even biting, and who felt they were just doing their jobs of guarding and protecting the family. The people started out wanting a dog to protect the family and property. They encouraged territorial behavior by outward approval or lack of correction, or they yelled at the dogs while inwardly being proud, which of course the dogs picked up.

They failed to clearly set the limits for the dogs on what constituted acceptable protective behavior. The dogs, generally intelligent and strong-willed individuals, increased their level of protection to aggressive behavior beyond the control of the person. Then, after continued lack of control or messages of secret approval, when these dogs were finally reprimanded for terrorizing or hurting people, they couldn't figure out what was wrong. They were just doing what they thought the person wanted.

The person who has animal companions has to take responsibility for setting reasonable rules. Some people find it acceptable to have animals only in certain parts of the house or for certain times of the day. Some allow animals on the furniture, and others don't.

The rules should be realistic for the animals. If the rules are quite unnatural, animals may not grasp why you would want them to behave that way—such as expecting dogs never to bark, or not providing a place for cats to scratch their claws and not allowing them to do so anywhere.

The liberties allowed and the rules to be followed need to be communicated to everyone concerned, both human and nonhuman, and consistently adhered to so that there is no confusion. Show your animal companions what you want. Remind them until they really get it. Be calm and communicative rather than impatient or violent. You are asking them to learn many things that are in varying degrees alien to their physical heritage. If you apply all the steps of communication described in this book, your animal companions will generally get what you mean and be willing to cooperate.

Once the rules have been fully understood and established, you need to be in control of the situation and of yourself when you correct a breaking of the rules. Flying off the handle in a tirade or being lax about letting the animal get away with it generally won't lead to harmony.

Let's say the cats pee on the carpet. A straightforward approach is to take them to the spot, firmly say "no," and put them in the litter box or wherever you want them to pee, praising them and making it pleasant for them to do the right thing. Ensure the litter is clean and in a location the cats find comfortable, or you are causing the broken rule; most cats do not like to use a smelly litter box or relieve themselves in uncomfortable or threatening situations. If the corrective action has to be repeated often—and you have thoroughly cleaned the area so that the stimulation of the smell is not allowed to tempt the cats to pee on the carpet again—you need to sit down with your cats for a two-way conversation to find the cause and clear it up with them.

They may be upset about some change in the household, and peeing is their way of registering disagreement. Listen to them, and resolve it as well as you can with communication and understanding. Then you can reinforce the rules and easily show your cat friends what you want them to do, as there will be no mental barrier in the way. Clear up the problem yourself or with the help of an animal communication specialist. You can then be strict and take the right amount of action necessary to get the message across and gain compliance.

You need to use common sense to create an orderly and harmonious environment. There is no one procedure that always works. "Punishment" varies according to the sensitivity of the individual, the degree of discipline necessary to make the point, and the severity of the infraction.

For most animals with whom you are really attuned, a look of disapproval is enough. A quiet but firm verbal reprimand, showing your animal friends what you are unhappy about and then repeating the positive thing that you expect of them, may be the right action. If you catch animals in the act, a tap on the rear and a firm "no" or quickly stopping them is appropriate.

Sometimes a denial of your presence, such as putting the animal outside or in another room, is the right action to enlist cooperation. Use only the amount of emphasis needed to show that their action is not okay and that you mean what you say. Only in extreme situations, where life is threatened, is violent action necessary.

Using strange, irrational methods to show animals they are wrong brings about misunderstanding, fear, or other negative feelings. An example of what I consider a weird method is what one animal psychologist recommended to a person I later consulted. To correct the cat for pooping on the couch, he told her to lock the cat in the drawer with his poop for a few hours. Instead of handling the problem, the cat became more confused and alienated, and the person became more frustrated. Not only did we have to work to clear the original upset causing the cat to poop in the wrong place, but also we had to handle the added problem of cruel treatment.

In some books on animal training, people are told to shove their cat's or dog's nose in their excrement when they relieve themselves in the wrong place, or jam it in their mouths (really!). I consider these actions stupid and ineffective, based on the irrational thinking of animals as automatons.

If a continued breaking of the rules occurs after using sensible methods of control and correction, there is something else aggravating the behavior. Perhaps the animals misunderstand something or are protesting, or some upset or fear or physical condition is causing them to lose control. If the underlying cause of misbehavior is not addressed, forcing animals to behave may be only a temporary solution or may lead to other neurotic behavior. It certainly isn't conducive to overall harmony. The source of the problem needs to be found and cleared up.

Sometimes a person's continued resistance or fear of the undesired behavior creates strong mental pictures that cause animals to act the fear out physically. For example, my male dog, Pasha, used to stand off and prepare to fight other male dogs. If I remained calm, keeping a neutral attitude about his meeting other dogs on a trail, and not putting a lot of attention on it, he generally would just sniff them and be on his way. If I grew fearful that he might get in trouble, and I projected that, he often started to run the macho trip, staring them down, hackles up.

What you think and feel definitely influences the responses of the animals and people who are close to you. Think about it.

If you do your best, even enlisting sound professional help, to clear up any underlying problem, and the misbehaving continues, it may be that it's become a habit that the animal finds comforting in some way. The remedy may require watchfulness and consistent handling or diversionary measures.

Know your animal friend. Use your common sense. Don't react with violent, strange, or extreme methods. You may need to tell your animal companions firmly that you've done all you can to clear things up, and now it's up to them to cooperate. If they don't you will . . .

Pick a disciplinary measure that is straightforward and that will get the message across with this individual. For example, it is often effective to put the animals outside or in a room away from the family until they realize their error and are ready to do their part. Communicate. Let your animal friends know what you're doing and why, and what you expect of them. Give them a chance to realize that breaking the rules doesn't work.

In most instances, doing this once or repeatedly for a moderate stretch of time will get through to the most hardened noncooperator. Don't overdo it and threaten animals with total banishment to start. Mean what you say. They'll get it, unless there has been so much previous conflict that they really don't want to be with you and would be happier somewhere else. It requires judgment. Give your animal friends and yourself the best deal.

For dogs, obedience training done with you is often a great way to make living with each other a team effort and fun. Brutal methods of dragging or jerking dogs around to get them to obey are not necessary. Enforced isolation, trickery, or any treatment that assumes dogs are unfeeling, unthinking things are not acceptable.

Make it a game, and apply the basic principles of communication outlined previously. Most dogs love obedience training, as long as it is done with a loving attitude. It brings them closer to you, helps them understand the rules of living with people, makes them feel more worthwhile, and fulfills their need to serve in a positive way.

These training principles can be applied to other animals besides dogs. Success depends on your patience and skill, your closeness to animals, and how willing and physically able they are to participate. Humans and their fellow animals have done amazing things in cooperation with each other.

YOUR ANIMAL
COMPANION'S VIEWPOINT

It's important to understand an animal's intention behind the behavior that you may consider strange or wrong. Don't punish animals for actions they consider favorable to you. Acknowledging and being responsive to your animal friend's purpose can work wonders. Let me give a few examples.

Tip, a mixed-breed dog, had acquired the habit of depositing his stools on a small rug in the living room. He had also started scattering or eating droppings from the cat litter box. His person had tried various methods to correct him, from yelling to pushing his face in it, but to no avail.

Tip's person told me it all started soon after she got a litter pan for the cats, when she had changed to having them indoors. I asked Tip to explain to me what was going on from his point of view. He had observed his person "playing" in the cat litter, scooping out the poop, and thought this was a great game. He liked the smell of the cats' leavings, and he thought that doing what his person did would please her.

He reasoned, since she made such a fuss over their poop, he'd make a present of his own where she'd be sure to see it and definitely know it was his gift and not theirs. He thought she'd enjoy scooping his poop as much as the cats.

It just didn't compute when she yelled at him for it. She never yelled at the cats. Oh well, he'd ignore it and continue giving her presents, as he was sure she'd be pleased soon.

This may sound stranger than fiction, and I'm often amazed at what animals communicate to me. However, it's common that when the intention behind an action is not understood, it's assumed, or at least hoped, that by repetition you'll catch on.

I handled this by fully understanding and acknowledging Tip. I explained his reasoning to his person, who laughed and was totally amazed and relieved to understand the situation. I had her thank Tip very thoroughly and sincerely for his intention. He then felt that his message was well received. I then explained to him what his person was doing with the cats' litter. He was not to relieve himself in the house, as this did not really please his person. She'd be pleased if he went outside as before.

To reinforce the acceptable action, I asked the person to praise her dog exuberantly when he went outside for the next few days. After a few reminders, he didn't leave a "present" on the rug again.

Here's a sad case where understanding and acknowledging might have saved an animal's life. I was conversing about animals with a woman I had just met in a restaurant. She told me about a young cat that a friend had given her. She and her husband had become quite fond of the cat until he started killing birds and bringing them home to eat. The woman thought this was horrible. No matter what she did to discourage the cat, he seemed to do it more, until he was bringing up to three birds home per day and not eating the cat food she gave him. It got to be too much for her. She felt such sympathy for the birds that she had her cat taken to the Humane Society to be killed.

While I understood the woman's feelings, this was a case of misunderstanding the cat's intention and not looking from his point of view. I have found that domesticated animals, who love you, try to please you in the ways that are very natural to them. It's very natural for cats to hunt. It's the finest expression of their genetic heritage. Cats may bring home their prey for you to show their pride and share it with you. They won't understand why you would be dismayed or punish them for it. It's like yelling at children for creating mud pies in your garden the first time that they discover how to do that and want to show you their creations. They won't understand if you're not pleased.

The thing to do with all communications from anyone is to understand what they are saying. In this case, the cat was probably proud of his hunting ability and wanted to show his person, thinking she'd be pleased.

When my cat, Peaches, and I first moved to the country, she used to present mice or birds at the foot of my bed in the morning. Although this was a shock to my bare feet, I did not scream and go "yuck." Instead, I thanked her wholeheartedly for the gift, really validating her ability as a huntress. When I was sure she really felt acknowledged, I asked her to take the body out of the house, or I'd take it out, explaining that I'd prefer if she kept her prey outside. She understood, and after a few times ceased to bring back dead or half-dead animals. If I had objected to her hunting in itself, I could have talked to her about that or put a bell on her collar to warn the birds or mice of her coming.

The woman in the restaurant mentioned that the cat seemed to get compulsive about it and do it more and more. Have you ever noticed that when you don't understand and acknowledge someone, they keep trying to get the message across somehow or prove it to you? Beings of all kinds generally mean well when they want their communications received and understood. Their messages can get desperate or weird when they have been ignored or rejected too often.

Your fears and mental pictures also help suggest to animals what is wanted, and so help create the situation. This woman had awful fears of dead or mauled birds each time she heard her cat outside the door. Perhaps she could have saved herself and her cat the pain and suffering by knowing and using this information.

I reviewed our conversation in the restaurant later and realized that this woman was eating chicken. She probably had never thought of the fact that she had indirectly killed a bird for her dinner. At least the cat was taking responsibility for killing his birds directly.

How many people would eat meat if they had to kill the cow or chicken or pig themselves? I doubt that this woman would. Yet, she had her cat killed (by someone else, of course) because he ate birds—something to think about.

While the present natural order of bodies consuming other animal or plant bodies for food may be revised sometime in the future, the reality now is that it is considered necessary or desirable for survival. Applying the principles of communication and understanding to this area would require that before you take plant or animal bodies for food, you get in communication with the beings animating the bodies and make an agreement regarding their providing food for you.

This has been the way of Native Americans and other tribal people. Native Americans approached the buffalo, or any life form they depended on, with respect and gratitude. They communicated with the spirits connected with those life forms and demonstrated how they would use the bodies to good purpose for their people's survival. The animal beings in most cases were probably willing to give their bodies in this arrangement. Their bodies weren't stolen or abused, and they, as spirits, could go peacefully on to their next lives as buffalo or other life forms.

Most of today's methods of animal farming and slaughter vary greatly from this ideal. There is often much deprivation of natural needs, lack of respect, cruelty, and no communication. Individuals have to judge for themselves the ethics of how they obtain food for their bodies and the responsibility they have in the matter. It's something to seriously consider.

When seeking to understand animal behavior, take a leap and try to see, hear, and generally perceive how the animal does. I literally look through their eyes and hear through their ears to get their side of the story. In lieu of this ability, get information on the animal through personal observation and research. Finding out the physical characteristics and genetic background of your particular kind of dog, cat, horse, or other animal can be very helpful. Don't rely on this alone, as animals combine their physical, mental, and spiritual qualities to come up with their own personalities and styles of approaching life.

To understand individuals fully, no method is better than stepping into their shoes—oops, paws! For example, one woman wanted to know why her terrier jumped around a lot in the car. He never seemed to sit still to look out the window as her larger dog did. She interpreted this as nervousness.

I looked through the little dog's eyes and saw how he saw. He could only encompass a section of the surrounding scene at a time, rather than having wide-angle vision. In order to catch as much as possible of the scenes going by while he rode in the car, he needed to jump around and move his head from place to place. At least that's how he handled it, and this may apply to other dogs who flit from position to position. Instead of assuming, I always check with individuals to see what's going on from their angles. I'm often surprised at the variations.

Another example of understanding from the animal's point of view was with my dog, Pasha. We visited New York City for the first time. He had been raised in Los Angeles, where he didn't have to walk along busy streets but spent most of his time in a large, tree-filled yard or on park or mountain trails. The noise in New York is deafening in comparison, as the crowded buildings echo the wall-to-wall traffic, which honks, screeches, and screams incessantly.

As we walked along, Pasha would suddenly whip around and snap or bite at his back. This was accentuated to near convulsive level when many cars beeped, and sirens screamed. I stopped, held him, and, hearing through his ears, found that the noise was percussively deafening, with a background drone as if a swarm of bees were attacking. The nerves through his spinal column were painfully registering the intense impulses. It was enough to drive anyone crazy.

I handled this sensory overload by pointing out where the individual noises were coming from as they occurred. As he started to locate the sources of the sounds, the cacophony began to sort out, and he could handle it better. Each time he jumped, I'd point out that the screech of brakes came from that truck, or the loud honk came from that van, and he would calm down. I also told him to tune down his hearing, as it was much too sensitive for the environment. He worked at that, and in a few days, he was no longer bothered by the street sounds and could calmly parade down the New York streets.

As a general handling of animals who are startled by something, it's good to point out or explain and have them see exactly what is causing the disturbance. This eliminates the fear that the source is something horrible that can't be confronted. This can prevent future negative reactions to the particular noise or sight.

Being able to assume an animal's viewpoint can also help you choose an animal companion that aligns with your needs and environment. It's a great way to handle any situation without resorting to a rote formula that isn't always applicable. It gives you the best source of information about your unique animal. I highly recommend cultivating it.

UPSETS BETWEEN ANIMALS

A common problem that people call me to handle is an upset or hostility between animals in a family. Individualized handling is best for each circumstance, but let me give a few examples and some basic guidelines.

Oro, a male Afghan pup, had developed the habit of being extremely possessive about his food. He would also force his sister, Zoya, away from her own food dish. They would sometimes fight over any scraps of food in the area. Except for this food issue, both dogs played together and generally got along famously.

At first, their people took the attitude that it was the dogs' own business and that they should sort it out themselves. This is comparable to letting two children slug things out and hurt each other without intervention. The dog fights became more frequent and sometimes very violent. Then the people tried yelling at the dogs loudly, and forcefully separating them while telling them this was not okay. This worked a bit better and often stopped the behavior, but did not prevent it from recurring. In fact, the habit seemed to grow more and more ingrained, and either pup now instigated and aggravated this unpleasant game.

I happened to be visiting once when both started a fight over some almost invisible piece of food. I grabbed both by the collar, separated them and said sternly, "That's it!" Both were totally immersed in the fight and continued to growl and try to get at each other. I held and shook them firmly and repeated loudly, "That's it!" Finally I got their attention. I lectured them calmly but firmly that their fighting was not okay and that they were to apologize to each other and would not be let go until this occurred.

Zoya quickly admitted that she had deliberately aggravated Oro to start the fight, and she apologized. Oro took longer to acknowledge his part in the matter but reluctantly apologized as well.

A thorough handling would include taking each animal individually, clearing up the original reason for the aberrant behavior, and ensuring they both took strict control over themselves so it never happened again. One should also encourage the accepted behavior by demonstration and praise.

With just this on-site handling, the problem diminished to almost nothing and was easily handled by the people when it did occur thereafter.

Whenever there is any misunderstanding among any of my animal friends, I always ensure that all parties take responsibility for their share in the action. They may need to be separated to cool down and think about it before you get a good conclusion with apologies and promises of good behavior. It must be taken to a full "happy ending" if you don't want the behavior to manifest again.

Get to the root of the upset on both sides, and handle it. A consensual solution and firm policy must be established, so that the situation doesn't repeat itself. This may include changing an environmental situation that contributed to the problem, such as the lack of individual food dishes or enough space, causing the animals to get in each other's hair—oops, fur! Listen to your animal friends' needs, and use your common sense.

Reiterate the animals' purposes as members of the family. Praise the desired behavior. Acknowledge animals for doing well. Ease up on your vigilance as the animals do what is required. Restore privileges if they had been curtailed as part of the handling.

There are times when you can let animals work things out themselves, and to some extent they must anyway. With just the right amount of good guidance, the process can go more smoothly and quickly. An example is when you get a new animal in the family. There may be a period where the new cat, dog, or bird is hissed or growled at or held aloof, until they communicate enough and establish their positions in relation to each other. Let them get to know each other in their own time. Intervene if the going gets too rough, and coach everyone through to understanding of their place or functions in the family.

Let the older animals know that they aren't being replaced and that you still love them. Consider the new arrival as the friend or playmate of the established animal family members instead of as your new animal companion. Emphasize this in your conversations with them. Tell the senior members you'd like them to look after and help the new animal become a good member of the family. Ask them to show the new animal the ropes. Tell them you're relying on them, because they are so reliable and intelligent. Admiration, sincerely given, helps to soothe hurt feelings or rough edges.

Show the new member, especially a young, eager animal, how to respect the rights of senior members and observe their needs. Curb too much exuberance in approaching senior animals, if this is unwanted by them. All family members must be secure in their places and encouraged to look after and contribute their specialness to each other. Once again, understanding, respect, and common sense apply.

Even dogs who normally chase cats and cats who normally chase birds can be taught to respect the other's right to live. Get them to look at each other as beings rather than bodies or prey, so they can learn to control the genetic urges to hunt the other. With some dogs this is easy. They will cuddle and fall asleep with the cat after a short introduction. Or the cat will be interested in but never attempt to pounce on the parakeet after a little coaching. Others will be tougher to handle. They may not want to control their genetic impulses, which may be stronger in them than in their gentler counterparts. They will not listen to you but prefer to enjoy the sensations of hunting and/or killing other animals.

Several difficult cases I have handled were dogs of mine. I adopted a female Afghan from the pound. Popiya ferociously went after the neighborhood cats when I first had her home. Each time she saw a cat, the picture of a leopard flashed in front of her face, and her eyes changed to the intense look of a huntress. The leopard picture was from her Afghan hound genetic heritage, since Afghans have been raised to hunt leopards in other parts of the world.

I handled it by catching her when the leopard image first flashed in front of her face upon seeing an ordinary cat. I would hold her and get her to see the real cat in front of her and face that cat as a spiritual being and not just as a cat body or prey. I'd say, "Look at that being," and acknowledge her when she did it, until she calmed down and didn't have to obey automatic responses. I'd then remind her firmly that she was not to chase cats or even think of killing them, as this was not acceptable to me or to the neighbors.

I later got my own cat companion, and in about a week, I could safely leave Popiya in the house alone with her without any problem. She never grew to love cats but mainly ignored them. My cat respected her and left her alone but was not afraid of her. She never chased cats again, and this is quite an accomplishment, considering her Afghan hound background.

An even tougher case was Miel, a female Afghan I raised from a pup. Pasha, my male, has always chased cats, but he loves them and has no intention to harm them. He just loves the chase. When he was a pup he listened to me when I asked him never to kill other animals. Once I saw Pasha catch a squirrel. He then let it go and bounced back, urging the stunned squirrel to run so Pasha could resume the chase.

Miel, however, had a strong huntress instinct in her that she was unwilling to release. She killed rats, mice, opossums, and birds, despite my instructing her as I did with Pasha. She was unwilling to listen to me on the subject, and I was never able to catch her in the act to stop her.

One day I caught her as she killed a cat. This upset me greatly. I shook her and whapped her rear to let her know that this was not okay and that I meant business. Then I left her alone for a few hours to let her think it over. After that we had a long talk about it, and she realized the wrongness of her action.

With her on the leash, we practiced looking at the cats in the neighborhood as beings and not just bodies, so that she could learn to control her instincts. She had a hard time releasing the pleasure of hunting and killing. Bringing cats into our own home enabled us to work on this daily at close range. After several months she was able to be around them without getting excited or having any intention to hurt them. She would stay calm and smell and lick them.

Later, when she thought no one was around, she tended to get fierce with the cats again, so I never could fully trust her alone with them, no matter what we did. To achieve the ideal of harmonious relationships among all animals is not always easy or even possible. It depends on your patience, good judgment, the strength of the animals' instincts, and, most of all, their willingness.

If I could have had cat companions when Miel was a puppy, perhaps it would have been easier to nip the aggression in the bud. My other Afghan, Rana, grew up among cats and easily learned how to play with them gently, though she chases after wild animals with huntress intentions. Each animal and situation is unique, and handling will be a bit different for each.

I've followed a similar procedure for reminding our cats to look at our finches, canaries, parakeets, and cockatiel as beings and to respect their rights. Cats are very much hunters, but many can be taught to master their instincts with members of the family and to channel their hunting urges in other ways.

I am against beating, electric rods, or other bizarre methods to shock animals into submission, as some animal trainers recommend. I have seen cases where this was considered the last resort, or the uncontrollable animal would have to be killed. It's difficult to decide what is best in these situations. Most animals do not start out with destructive intentions toward others but become that way through abuse and deprivation.

Brutal training methods generally instill a neurotic fear or apathy in the animal. The animals are never consciously and reliably in control. Of course, this is alien to respecting and appealing to a being's choice, intelligence, and spiritual nature. Good, firm control of wild or reactive animals is necessary. Brutality is not.

In handling animals, you need to balance your awareness of them as infinitely capable spiritual beings (as we all are) with how they manifest as individuals in their physical form. It's tricky sometimes to understand how your incredible animal friend can sometimes do silly things as a dog, but then the same applies to humans. Deal with animals as fellow beings, with an understanding of their composite physical/spiritual nature. Let's foster an attitude of mutual cooperation and respect.

WILD ANIMALS

A woman wrote to me, "I need help in understanding the behavior of my cat. He was born in a meadow near Solvang (California). His mother was wild—belonged to no one. He is seven years old now and has always attacked us at our ankles and hands. . . . When he is on one of our laps and we are rubbing him, and he seems so content, he'll suddenly snap at the hand that pets (and feeds) him! We have had this kitty since he was six weeks old."

Situations like this occur when people attempt to domesticate a wild animal or handle an animal that is very afraid around humans. To understand what is happening, one of the first things to look at is the genetic makeup of the animal.

Wild animals are geared for instant reactions to any stimulus that signals a threat to their survival. Their senses are highly tuned to noise, moving objects, and smells, and they are instantly ready to flee, hide, or attack. They cannot stop to deliberate whether the stimulus is coming from a friendly source, because in the wild, hesitation may mean death.

Even slow, apparently friendly or harmless movements from other animals, including humans, may have turned into death-dealing blows in their past. The survivors have learned to react first, get into a safe position, and then, if there is opportunity, to study the assailant's motives or interests. Their behavior may not seem rational to us when they are transferred to a tamer environment, unless we understand that the animal is still geared for survival in an environment filled with potential dangers.

Living with humans, animals gradually become accustomed to human motions and surroundings, if the environment is made calm and secure for them. They learn that it is not necessary to flee or fight every movement. However, their genetically inherited tendencies may make them skittish at unfamiliar movements. Their sensory mechanisms may still be in "high gear," making a small movement of the hand appear like a blow aimed directly at their bodies.

Because of body sensitivity, certain pitches of sound may deal agonizingly sharp signals through their heads or spines that make them jump, twitch, or bite. A change in the person's body chemistry or emotional energy may put them on alert.

In the case of the cat mentioned above, even though he was brought into the person's home at six weeks old, he was already too influenced by his background to relax all the time around humans. His mother may have carefully taught him the way to survive in the world. He may have gone through some painful experiences if he disobeyed the necessity for alertness. So, even after seven years of human handling, he still harks back to his early training when something strikes these survival mechanisms.

Some motion, sound, smell, or other sense, unnoticeable to people, may alert his body to danger, even though in his domesticated circumstances, that danger is not there. He may not always react that way, depending on how secure he is in the present environment or whether his learned experience or genetic makeup is influencing him.

He may be sitting in his person's lap, totally enjoying the warmth and affection, and suddenly he reacts unconsciously to something in the area that reminds him of some danger in the past. The person's touch is then overstimulating to him, or may even trigger feelings of being trapped or the need to be alert. Reactive impulses such as this can be found in many animals, including humans.

To fully handle the situation, some animals may need individual counseling of their fears and the sources of their erratic behavior, or months of environmental conditioning by a sensitive, patient person. While each condition and animal's response is individual, there are some actions you can take with a wild or fearful animal to enable you to coexist more happily.

The first requirement is to make a safe, quiet space. There should be no extraneous noises or distractions. Your movements should be slow and deliberate. Speak calmly and slowly, and explain what you are going to do next, visualizing it clearly. Sudden moves or changes startle. Be quietly present where the animal can watch you. Don't threaten by trying to get close when they are afraid or hostile. Let them have the chance to feel safe enough to accept your presence and make a friendly approach toward you. Let them get to know you—your body, your way of moving (slowly), your voice, your smell—and to sense that you have no intention to harm or trap. Withdraw from their area when they seem to have progressed a little in being comfortable with you around. Don't overdo the initial encounters.

In the case of the cat mentioned earlier, the people had already established a rapport with him, but he may have been reacting to something they were doing. Being rubbed mechanically or too long can act as a physical energy drain or irritation. You may have experienced this when someone has caressed your body absent-mindedly. It can be even more annoying to a very sensitive animal. Always handle animals consciously with the intention to increase harmony. They will respond to your intention and begin to trust you, if your actions don't threaten them.

Once you have animals trusting you in their surroundings, you can slowly reach for them by moving your body closer. If they react badly, then withdraw slowly, and let them have their own space again. Don't react with sudden motions, scolding, or punishment. You'll defeat the purpose of making them feel safe around you, and you may unconsciously remind them of past threats.

After the period of getting to know you at a distance, your animal friends may start to tentatively reach for you or climb in your lap. Let them explore and get used to you, but don't force them to stay. When they feel safe enough to let you touch them, put your hand on their body slowly but firmly. Don't poke fingers at them or touch with feathery strokes (unless you are working with a very small body, such as an insect). This can stimulate their sensory apparatus and make them feel jumpy, or they may attack you. Establish physical communication with them by gradually lifting your hand and placing it gently but firmly on part of their body. Start with the more acceptable areas like the upper back, until they are more comfortable with your hand, and gradually move to other parts. Mentally or verbally communicate soothing, empathetic thoughts. End your time with the animals when they are calmer or happier, not running away or attacking you. If they do react negatively, withdraw calmly, return to quiet behavior until they are calmer, and then leave them alone.

You don't want to force animals to do anything that is too frightening for them. Once you have established enough trust to handle them physically, if they get jumpy during your contact, you may hold them until they calm down before you let them go. Don't overdo your handling, and don't underdo it.

Good handling requires discretion, sensitivity, experience, a loving, patient attitude, and a willingness to closely observe and understand animals' responses. A lot depends on your attitude, which animals perceive. If you intend to help them and not force them to do things, they will feel safer with you and make more progress. If you do not have their best interests at heart, they will be aware of this and respond negatively. Do not try to "conquer" wild animals, but work for increased understanding and learning on both sides.

Regard it as a privilege to get in close contact and establish a good relationship with wild animals. The rewards of mutual trust between human and nonhuman animals are among the finer things in life.

Some people may worry that the approaches outlined here may result in injury to human handlers. Obviously, you don't want animals to harm you or others during your attempts to familiarize them with you and your surroundings. If animals are likely to attack while you are working with them, keep a fence or wire enclosure between you, in a way that still allows a comfortable space and connection for both of you. A lot of communication can occur without bodily contact.

Later, when animals feel comfortable most of the time with human company, any lapses into wild behavior can be taken up and handled as you might with other members of the family. Just reprimanding some animals by pointing out that their actions are not acceptable is enough to enlist their cooperation. You may communicate with the animals and find out what upset them, or observe what upset them and handle that with understanding of their viewpoint. You may see that they do not really perceive you when they exhibit the wild-eyed or glazed look that goes along with a dangerous environment. In that case, you can have them look at the objects in the environment by pointing them out one at a time. This gets them to see their present surroundings and calms them down so they can relate to you in the present again.

At times, some animals, just as some humans, need a certain amount of force to contain their bodies when they are being wild. This puts you in control of the situation, so that they can calm down enough to control their bodies. It takes good observation and judgment to see what kind of action will work best with animals at each moment. Violence is generally not rehabilitative for animals. It can cause distrust and the desire to get back at you, though it may be necessary for handling a situation that is too dangerously out of control to evoke the animal's attention and proper action by milder means.

I had a terrific experience with handling one wild animal. I was living in a cabin behind a house in a large, woodsy yard, and I would leave the cabin door ajar for my dogs to go in and out when

I was not home. Once, when I returned from an errand, my dogs greeted me at the house, but as we neared the cabin they raced in, leaping and barking at the space beneath a small cabinet. I pulled them out to see what was there and found a baby opossum, looking very stiff and dead.

After urging the dogs outside, I crouched down near the opossum and told him I knew he was alive, so he didn't have to pretend anymore. He flashed his eyes at me distrustfully. I softly explained to him that he couldn't stay in the cabin, and that we had to get him safely outside without the dogs attacking him.

I got a paper bag and told him that I wanted him to get inside, visualizing him inside the bag with me carrying him to safety over the fence to a neighbor's yard. I detailed exactly what I wanted him to do, especially that he was not to bite me. I assured him that I would not hurt him or let the dogs get him. He stayed where he was, eyeing me with intense suspicion, so I withdrew the bag and again explained the situation to him. I told him he really had no choice but to trust me. The dogs, barking and scratching outside, would get him if I didn't help him out, so he'd better get into the bag.

He looked at me warily, but this time when I put the bag down, he crawled into it. I tipped the bag up and folded the top over, explaining what I was doing each step of the way and that he'd be okay. As I opened the door, my excited dogs leaped into the cabin, following his smell and former presence. I held the bag high, closed the door, and proceeded to the fence. I told the opossum that I would open the bag, and he was not to bite me but to jump out into the neighbor's yard and not return here. He sped out and disappeared into the ivy.

This was my first experience with an opossum. My success was due to making the area as safe as possible for him, assuring him slowly and calmly that I could be trusted, and telling him clearly what I wanted him to do. I did not put him in the position where he had to bite me, and I enlisted his cooperation by quiet communication, clearly visualizing the situation for him and ensuring the dogs would not harm him. In that short encounter, we reached an understanding, and both of us had a good experience.

Another part of making the wild or reactive animal's environment safe, predictable, and calming is conscious handling of nutritional needs. A diet as close to natural as possible is best; I'll cover this in the next chapter. Some common herbs that have natural calming properties and can be put into your animal's food or water (fresh, powdered, or brewed as tea) are chamomile, hops, red clover, peppermint, rosemary, sage, valerian, lobelia, marshmallow root, skullcap, or wild cherry. Also important are sufficient exercise, fresh air, and sunlight, without which any animal (including humans) can become nervous, irritable, or ill.

Don't be alarmed or dismayed if your wild animal friend does not respond immediately to your offers of trust and understanding. Some animals, like some people, do not want to change and will resist your attempts to communicate with them. Allow them to be the way they are. You cannot enforce their response to your help. Sometimes, just by withdrawing, the animal will then get interested and desire more connection. For the animal who wants to change, you should see a good response in a short time with the methods offered here.

SUMMARY OF PRINCIPLES

It's impossible to prescribe a specific handling for every possible behavior problem or attempt to explain the wide range of animal behavior, to which many volumes are devoted. However, here is a summary of principles that can be creatively applied to any situation:

- Know your animals' physical and emotional needs and understand how that relates to your coexistence.

- Be able to look at things through the animals' eyes. See and include their viewpoint when making or enforcing rules. Be accepting and be real.

- Clearly communicate what you'd like. Tell and show your animal friends, and ensure they understand what you mean, step by step.

- Be consistent. Repeat demonstrations as necessary until the animals really grasp it, without overtiring them in one period of time.

- Be loving and honest in your approach. Have respect for the animal and yourself.

- Acknowledge and praise acceptable behavior.

- If you have to say "no" to stop an undesired action, give your animal friends something positive to do that you can praise. Leave them on a positive note, and use the "no's" sparingly.

- Keep calm when correcting animals. Screaming or inflicting pain is almost always unnecessary and can lead to neurotic reactions.

- Clear up the cause behind the misbehavior to reestablish mutual understanding.

- Use common sense, and don't be rote in your approach. Use what works and leads to more harmony in the long run.

PHYSICAL

needs and

Behavior

Problems

SOMETIMES I'VE BEEN CALLED upon to help an animal with a behavior problem or illness that seems to be mentally caused or prolonged, but it doesn't totally resolve through communication and counseling around the animal's associated upsets or traumatic experiences. Skin disorders, arthritis, hyperactivity, epilepsy, diarrhea, listlessness, shyness, and a host of other problems are often brought on by mental or emotional factors, but the physical elements of nutritional deficiencies and environmental stress should also be addressed for a stable recovery. They are so important that I advise looking for and handling them first.

Drugs may suppress the symptoms, but they do not eradicate the mental or physical roots as counseling or proper nutrition can. At best, drugs help in emergencies to relieve pain and jog the body into mustering all its efforts to survive. At worst, they create side effects that further weaken the animal's overall health and future survival.

I was called to see a dog who had been diagnosed several months previously by a veterinarian as epileptic and given drugs to handle the condition. His person worried, as the dog was becoming apathetic, moping around most of the time. While he did not have any convulsions, he also no longer had the old sparkle in his eyes or interest in activity. His skin was becoming very dry, and his hair was beginning to fall out.

The person first noticed the dog having fits after she came back from a vacation. The dog communicated to me how it had been a shock for him to have his person leave. The person that had been left in charge was hostile and would yell at him and lock him inside the bedroom if he barked. He was left alone for many hours, not knowing when his person or anyone else would return. After we helped clear the upset through communication, the dog brightened up considerably, wagging his appreciation to his person and me.

For the dog's physical well-being, I recommended that he be fed an additive-free diet of cooked whole grains, fresh meat, and vegetables, supplemented with nutritional yeast, dolomite (calcium-magnesium), bone meal, cod-liver oil, and vitamins B-complex, E, and C, all of which would help calm his nerves and restore his physical balance. (Dosages can be found in the books written by veterinarians, cited later in this chapter.)

This enabled his person to slowly reduce the drug dosage prescribed for epilepsy. In less than three weeks, the dog was off the drugs, with no relapse into convulsions. He soon returned totally to his former perky attitude.

Here are some general recommendations for animal (mainly dog and cat) care that can help prevent illness and behavior problems:

- Provide fresh air, natural light, plenty of exercise, clean and safe quarters, warmth, loving communication, and understanding.

- Avoid commercially processed foods with artificial preservatives, flavoring and coloring, refined sugar in all its forms (brown sugar, dextrose, sucrose, corn syrup, etc.), junk foods, most canned foods, and overfeeding.

- Allow your animal companion to fast and drink liquids and eat grass when not feeling well. This is the natural way for the animal's body to flush out toxic materials and heal itself. Don't urge animals to eat or force-feed them unless advised to do so in treatment of a specific disease under the care of a nutritionally informed veterinarian.

- Encourage a mainly raw-food diet, as close as possible to what the animal would consume in the wild.

Contrary to what many people assume about carnivores, they do not subsist only on animal flesh. When they kill another animal for food, they first consume the stomach and intestines, which contain partially digested vegetables and grains, then other internal organs, blood, cartilage, bones, and skin. They also eat grass, roots, herbs, fruit, nuts, and eggs.

Canned or cooked meat, if fed too often, tends to decay in their intestines and leave toxic residues, which can create a great breeding ground for parasites and contribute to body malfunction. Use mainly raw or lightly cooked meat (organic if possible), or no meat at all if your dog or cat is one of those that thrives well on a vegetarian diet. It may be dangerous to maintain a cat on a non-meat diet, since they need the amino acid, taurine, found only in flesh food.

Other valid protein sources that can be used are raw marrow-bones, lightly cooked fish, cottage and hard cheese, yogurt, tofu, nuts, nut butters, and soybean products. For cats, which have higher protein needs than dogs, this should comprise 60 to 80 percent of the diet, and for dogs, 25 to 40 percent. Raw and steamed vegetables help rid the body of toxins and supply a balance of vitamins, minerals, and enzymes, and can be 10 to 25 percent of the diet. Whole grains (brown rice, oatmeal, wheat, millet, etc.)—soaked, sprouted, or cooked to aid digestibility—or chemical-free kibble (dry food) will supply many nutritional needs and the bulk of the diet: 50 percent for dogs and 10 to 20 percent for cats. Fruit and nuts in moderation are great for snacks.

- Add food supplements to counteract the effects of environmental pollution, devitalized foods, poor health, and the considerable strain of living with humans, and to ensure that all nutritional needs are supplied. Use nutritional yeast, cod-liver oil, kelp, alfalfa and other green food powder or tablets, bone meal, and cold-pressed vegetable oil. Add zinc, lecithin, and B-complex vitamins if there are any skin problems and vitamin C for prevention and healing of any detrimental health condition. Vary the dosage according to body size and need, consulting the following references:

Dr. Pitcairn's Complete Guide to Natural Health for Dogs and Cats, by Richard H. Pitcairn, D.V.M., and Susan Hubble Pitcairn. Emmaus, Pa.: Rodale Press, 1982. This is a detailed reference on holistic care for dogs and cats, helping you to prevent and treat ailments using gentle, natural methods—a must for the well-informed animal person.

The Complete Herbal Book for the Dog, by Juliette de Bairacli Levy. New York: Arco Publishing, Inc., 1971.

Herbal Handbook for Farm and Stable, by Juliette de Bairacli Levy. Emmaus, Pa.: Rodale Press, Inc., 1976.

How to Have a Healthier Dog, by Wendell O. Belfield, D.V.M., and Martin Zucker. Garden City, N.Y.: Doubleday & Co., Inc., 1981.

The Very Healthy Cat Book, by Wendell O. Belfield, D.V.M., and Martin Zucker. New York: McGraw-Hill, 1983.

There are a number of other books on different aspects of animal treatment with herbs, homeopathy, diet, and other healing modalities, but these are some of my favorite ones. They will help you understand how to supply a more natural environment and diet, which in turn may help clear up a lot of behavior and health problems.

Reaching for that canned or dry commercial dog or cat food may be convenient. Realize that you may be setting your animal up for future illness, strain, or strange behavior because of the unfit-for-human-consumption leftovers from the slaughter-house and toxic additives that this convenience food often contains. The extra time and care it takes to feed a close-to-natural diet are worth the savings in veterinary and animal communication specialist (!) bills, plus avoiding headaches, worry, or guilt for yourself. Consider it your animal health insurance.

SPAYING AND NEUTERING

People often ask me how their animal friends feel about being spayed or neutered. Most of the companion animals I have communicated with about the subject, including cats, dogs, horses, rabbits, goats, cows, and sheep, are relieved and happy to have their sexual urges and reproductive cycles out of the way, if these hormonal flows interfere with their ability to fulfill their purpose in being with their human friends. How could this be, you may ask, since having their reproductive organs intact is their natural state?

Beings who consciously choose to become companion animals generally do so to love, serve, and enjoy their human companions in the best way they are able. Wild animals generally avoid humans and have their own societies exclusive to their kind. Domesticated animals usually seek human company and consider humans their families. They even have friends of other species, with whom they would not normally associate in their wild state.

Many animals have told me how they came here to serve certain people by giving them devotion and teaching them about unconditional love and full enjoyment of life. While they may enjoy the company of their own species, many of these animals desire human company more. They consider that they and their people belong with each other. They feel frustration, resentment, fear, or distraction when sexual hormones dictate that they pursue a mate, or when the opposite-sex animal pursues them, if this pulls them away from their main purpose for being a companion animal.

Another reason for having animals altered is so that animals of the opposite sex can be companions to each other without the stress of mating behavior and constant reproduction. Stallions are often lonely and pent up, because, in most equestrian facilities, they have to be kept away from other horses, except when breeding. Many are relieved that they can be closer to other horses and people after they are gelded (neutered).

Georgie, a Netherland dwarf rabbit companion of mine, loved being with his mate, Elfie. I separated them after they had two litters, as it was hard to find good homes for the babies. Georgie, normally sweet-tempered, was furious with me for taking him away from Elfie, even though I had explained why I did that, and he could touch and communicate with her through a wire cage. I told him if he wanted to be with Elfie, he'd have to be neutered, which would mean he couldn't mate with her anymore. He wanted to be with her very much and agreed to the operation. It took Elfie awhile to stop expecting and encouraging Georgie to mate with her, but they cuddled and groomed each other and were so happy to be together again.

Altering is best done when an animal is young, just after puberty. They quickly recover from the surgery and don't have to contend with the confusions or habits from past sexual behaviors. Several of my animal friends have thanked me for having them spayed, after they had experienced the conflicting feelings of their first heats.

People too often identify themselves with their animal companions, and flinch at the thought of being "neutered." Women may feel it would be wonderful for their dog to have babies, to experience the joys of motherhood. Men, fearing even the idea of castration, may adamantly refuse to have their dog neutered. They may even enjoy their dog's aggression toward other dogs, and fear that neutering will turn their dog into a "lazy wimp."

Your animal companion is not the same as you. Animal sexual behavior is largely determined by hormonal cycles. Humans generally have a choice about following their sexual prompting. Except for a few unusual individuals, other animals do not. This creates a conflict for companion animals. They want to be with their people. The mating urges may cause behavior considered undesirable by humans, such as running away, fighting other animals of the same sex and getting injured, territorial marking, yowling and climbing up the walls, females being pursued by male animals, hyperactivity, or aggression.

A woman with a female Irish setter wanted to know why her dog was having false pregnancies and acting very strange after her heat cycles. I have heard veterinarians and professional dog breeders recommend that a dog who has false pregnancies be spayed, as it often signals future reproductive problems. This person felt that having her dog "spaded," as she called it, would be unnatural. Perhaps even this common mispronunciation of the word *spayed* conjures fears of something gruesome, like surgery done with a spade!

The Irish setter came over, leaned against me, and sighed, asking me to hold her. She was having a very difficult time telling me that she didn't want puppies. She didn't want to disappoint her person, who she knew wanted her to have puppies. She got emotionally upset every time she came into heat, and her body reacted wildly. How could she tell her person that she just wanted to be a devoted and loving companion to her? Would her person accept that?

This was a case of a person projecting her own desires for motherhood onto her dog and making the dog's life miserable. I relayed the dog's feelings to the person and hoped she would do what was best for her dog and have her spayed.

Many people work hard at getting their dogs pregnant, without success, and call me to find out the reason. The female dogs often tell me how having puppies is not for them, and they resist the whole breeding process. Many who do get pregnant do not enjoy it and reject their puppies. Others get reproductive disorders. This seems to be nature's message that these dogs were not meant to be bred. Perhaps many domesticated animals are losing their ability to reproduce, because there is such a surplus of homeless dogs and cats.

People often breed their dogs because they or their friends want a dog just like their Coco or Max. It is natural to believe your wonderful animal friend is the best around. There is no guarantee that the offspring will be images of the parents. Many of the characteristics you love about your animal friend are not hereditary but spiritual qualities of that individual. In my work, I have met thousands of incredible animals. Beings of wonderful character seem to make their way into the world one way or another and they all need homes. So it's not up to you to boost the supply of baby animal bodies.

One person wanted to breed her adored golden retriever, despite evidence of hip dysplasia and arthritis, even as a young animal. What can justify the suffering of physical deformity consciously passed on through generations? Wild animals must be strong and fit to survive and breed. People who breed animals must be responsible for mating only those with outstanding health, temperament, constitution, and freedom from hereditary defects. Following whims or fashions in breeding, without regard for overall fitness, can lead to disaster.

People will also say they have homes lined up for all the puppies or kittens. There are estimated to be 25 million homeless cats and dogs born in the United States yearly. About 15 million are killed or donated to research by animal shelters. The rest suffer disease, starvation, or brutal injury and death on the streets or back roads. Each animal who finds a home has a counterpart who didn't get one.

Spaying and neutering end the emotional and physical turmoil caused by hormonal cycles. Altering does not take away animals' zest for life or make them lazy. It makes animals less prone to the hormone-related diseases of unneutered animals, and usually helps them to live longer.

So, for ethical, humane, behavioral, and emotional reasons, it is best to spay and neuter most companion animals. The general consensus from the viewpoints of the animals themselves is that they are happier that way.

COMMUNICATION WITH FLEAS?

I'm taking up this topic here because people often ask me at lectures, in jest or in desperation, "Can you communicate with and do anything about fleas (or flies, bees, ticks, mosquitoes, etc.)?"

Fleas can be a source of much physical and emotional strain for animals (including humans). Since I've done a lot of research and given much time to handling them, I'll share with you some of my discoveries.

What emotion or image do these hardy, parasitic invaders conjure up? You may experience anything from rage to despair at the thought of these seemingly nasty creatures sucking the blood from your beloved animal companion, causing you both untold physical and mental torture. What can be done to handle them? Solutions range from scattering eucalyptus buds and branches around the house to nuclear warfare. The latter would probably just cause fleas, like cockroaches, to flourish.

What do I do about my animals' fleas? Cry, sweat, scream, and scratch! Actually, I've tried a number of methods with varying degrees of success. I'll list most of the remedies I've tried or heard of and explain their positive and negative aspects, and then conclude with my most "far out" or spiritual method.

Chemical Poisons. Flea dips, shampoos, powders, sprays, collars, bombs, or professional extermination kill or stun fleas on contact, but have the disadvantages of also being to a greater or lesser degree toxic to other life forms, such as dogs, cats, and people. Some animals, especially cats, have bad reactions to the poisons, which may be deadly if they overload the organs of elimination (liver, kidneys, lungs, intestines, skin), and if the chemicals accumulate in the body. It might be wise to avoid prolonged use or using them at all if you or your animal friend have a detrimental health condition, which these treatments may aggravate. You might also want to stick to the safer flea potions, such as those containing pyrethrums.

Obviously, you want to bring relief to your animal buddies, as fleas can cause severe irritation and reactions. Most poisons do not handle flea eggs, which will recreate the cycle of infestation when hatched, unless you repoison your area and animals every few weeks or less. It is a great relief to have a flea-free animal and environment. Weigh the benefits against the disadvantages. There is other, less toxic handling.

Cleaning. Flea eggs, larvae, and adult fleas are very resistant to being washed or swept away but can be vacuumed up in the house daily or as often as possible, to help fight the battle of reinfestation and multiplication. Vacuuming is one of the most effective indoor means, with no harmful side effects to animals or humans. Throw the bag away after use, or vacuum up some flea powder or diatomaceous earth before you put the vacuum cleaner away, if you don't want fleas to propagate and crawl out again.

Another method is to sprinkle salt or borax powder on the carpets, floors, and grounds, as well as on, under, and behind furniture and animal bedding, and leave it on for one or two days. After you vacuum, resprinkle the salt or borax. These ingredients dry out the flea eggs and larvae, stopping the flea reproduction cycle. Persist for several months to completely rid the home of fleas. Diatomaceous earth (use the natural, unprocessed kind, not the kind for pool filters), which dries out flea bodies, can also be sprinkled, but it's messy indoors.

Grooming. Brushing and combing help to keep your animals flea-free, if you are vigilant and use a fine flea comb to catch the fleas. Dropping the little culprits in water to which a bit of detergent has been added will handle them before they jump away. This can be hard work, especially with a long-haired animal. Nevertheless, combined with environmental handling, it's very effective.

Avoidance. Keep animals out of flea-infested areas, like ivy, fields, and your yard. This limits animals' activity and access to fresh air and natural light—an undesirable aspect of this approach.

However, if you can keep your house well vacuumed and your animal companions well groomed, they don't have a chance to pick up any more fleas.

Herbal Aids. There are many: herbal flea collars, herbal flea powder, eucalyptus leaves or buds, fresh fennel or bay leaves sprinkled around bedding, ground cloves, oils of eucalyptus, citronella, pennyroyal, vetiver, rue, camphor, clove, orange, lemon, sassafras, verbena, mustard, thyme, anise, lavender, pine wood, sage, cardamom, cedarwood. Singly or in combination, herbal oils rubbed into the animal's coat, added to shampoos or bathwater, and sprayed around the bedding, carpet, and floors, help repel fleas. Cedar shavings or oil can also be used in bedding. Herbal flea powders can be dusted on rugs, floors, and grounds.

Herbal repellant shampoos and dips, most of which contain citrus oils, can remove fleas and soothe irritated skin. You can make your own dip to apply to the animal's skin by steeping a thinly sliced whole lemon in a pint of near boiling water overnight. Others recommend a mixture of apple cider vinegar and water.

I like the smell of most herbal oils, especially citronella or citrus, but some people and animals do not. The oils can irritate the skin if overused in too strong a concentration. They protect you and your animal friends from fleas for various durations, generally brief, depending on the amount of exposure to heavy infestation and the hardiness of fleas in your area. You can get most of these oils, or sprays and shampoos containing them, at well-supplied natural food, drug, and pet stores.

You can also plant insect-repellant plants around your yard. Besides the ones mentioned above, from which oils are extracted, you can try garlic, onion, the chinaberry tree, the fernlike ant-eater plant, and shoofly (*Nicandra physolodes*).

Mechanical Aids. There are ultrasonic devices that emit high frequency sounds, inaudible to humans, which are supposed to keep insects and rodents away or disorient them so they cannot reproduce. Some people report their effectiveness in chasing fleas from indoors. They do not seem to affect fleas already on the animal or picked up again outside, unless such an ultrasonic device is worn around the neck. They may have subtle negative effects on humans and other animals, but further research is needed.

There is a flea trap that you can buy for use in your home at night to attract fleas to a light and catch them on a sticky pad. You can make your own version by filling a shallow plate or pan with soapy water and setting a 25-watt bulb or high intensity lamp next to the pan, shining the light over the water. Fleas jump toward the light, and fall into the soapy water and drown. Don't use plain water, as the fleas can float and jump out. Use regularly in various rooms during flea season, and you can rid your home of fleas. This is certainly a nontoxic method that has the advantage of working while you sleep.

Nutritional Aids. A fresh, natural, unprocessed diet, including raw, finely chopped vegetables to keep your animals' insides clean and healthy, helps to prevent flea attraction. Nutritional yeast, B-complex vitamins (especially B-1), and fresh grated garlic or garlic oil added to the diet can build animal resistance and aid in flea repulsion. They have no harmful side effects, unless the animal is allergic to them.

Some holistic veterinarians and animal nutritionists find that proper nutrition is the foremost preventive of flea infestation. Healthy animals create their own immunity to fleas and other parasites. Parasites are most attracted to weak, unhealthy, or very young animals. Treatment that strengthens the immune system helps to rid animals of fleas. Devitalized commercial food, flea poisons, or any kind of environmental poisons weaken the animal, and in the long run can increase susceptibility to fleas.

Animals differ in their constitutional makeup and their resistance to fleas. For some, nutritional supplements seem to handle the flea problem, while for others, these supplements by themselves seem inadequate, and you may have to use a ariety of methods. Attentions to diet, grooming, exercise, and mental and emotional well-being all contribute to a healthy, flea-free animal.

Prevention is the best line of defense. Once there is a heavy flea infestation, the patient, persistent, and thorough use of a compendium of approaches may be needed. When I lived in a heavily flea-infested area of Los Angeles, despite the home-made diet, the supplements, and all the good care my animal companions received, we still had to resort to a variety of means to keep the flea population in check. The payoff: I noticed that my animals seemed not to scratch much or be tormented by fleabites, nor did they develop the skin problems and allergies that I saw in many of the animals in my practice.

Spiritual Approach. One summer, after using just about all of the natural, nonpoisonous remedies and some chemical solutions, I still waged the battle with fleas. I decided to try to communicate with the fleas to understand their viewpoint better and to enlist their cooperation in not devouring my dogs and cats.

The message I got from them was "I'm hungry," no matter what I said or asked of them. Perhaps I caught them at mealtime, and they had too much attention on food! I got the idea this was a nonstop recording, so I lost patience and shelved that approach.

I then decided to stop my resisting and trying to get rid of them, and attempted instead to assume their viewpoint and accept their right to exist. I imagined myself being all the fleas in the area, hopping up and down with millions of tiny black bodies, enjoying biting warm mammals. As I did that and totally eliminated my resistance to them, I felt them disappear from my area. It was incredible, as I had been swatting them from my legs a minute before, and now there were none around.

The catch was that my dogs did not also do the same, so the fleas persisted for them. My dogs did not feel a pressing need to stop fighting fleas. It gave them something to do when there was nothing more interesting happening. I noticed that they rarely scratched when they were having fun on a trail or at the beach, only when boredom set in.

The flea-free state did not last, because I did not constantly maintain my state of nonresistance, and there were other people around who continued to hate and resist fleas. I found I could duplicate it for myself when necessary. The trick is in overcoming or not being influenced by others' resistance.

This principle may have a wide application to other areas of life that "bug" you. Try it.

OTHER INSECTS

Communicating sincerely with other insects that bother you, such as flies, bees, cockroaches, or ants, can yield harmonious results. I've had some great personal experiences and results with clients, by approaching insects as intelligent beings with whom you can cooperate.

After I've listened to the insects' reasons for doing what they do and agreed to help them meet their needs, I've asked them kindly to leave my food or work areas when needed, and received immediate cooperation. You can address them as individuals or talk to the "boss" or spirit in charge of their group or species (sometimes referred to as the oversoul).

The most important element is your attitude. Nonresistance and the willingness to listen to and really see their viewpoint and to work out a mutually acceptable solution are vital. As repulsive as insects may be regarded, they are just fellow beings of different forms, with their own purposes, emotions (yes, they have emotions), and social interactions. In fact, if you really get inside a colony of social insects, like bees and ants, you'll find they are more like humans than most other animals— amazingly so. You may find, as you get to know them without prejudice, that you no longer feel the need to repel them but instead get along just fine alongside them in this world.

One interesting experience I had that illustrates insects' nature as thinking beings happened when I was outdoors meditating. A fly kept landing on my hand, and after a few attempts at shooing her away, I decided to talk with her. I brought her close to my face and told her that if she wanted to keep touching me, then I would like to touch her. I felt her surprise that a human was talking to her. She stayed long enough to let me gently touch her back with my finger, and then she flew away. She quickly returned, and we repeated this game about five times. It was incredible to feel her fuzzy back!

I could feel her wonder about me and her trust. She left with a different attitude about people, or at least about one person. It was a wonderful experience for both of us. I kept in telepathic touch with her as she went her way and told some of her fly companions what happened. Just as humans might be, they were incredulous, obviously wary from their experience of humans as dangerous, insensitive creatures.

It's always wonderful to get that shift of viewpoint when you communicate to another species, especially one that is normally closed off from understanding because of human preconceptions. Harmony and oneness with all beings become a nearer reality.

HELP IN INJURY AND ILLNESS

Besides the natural health and first aid treatments that appear in the references cited earlier, and veterinary care as needed, there are other methods you can use to help an animal recover more quickly and fully from illness and injury.

Some physical techniques require considerable training to master, like acupuncture and chiropractic. Others can be learned from books or short courses, such as acupressure or foot reflexology. I'd like to pass on some simple techniques that I have learned in my training as a health educator for people, which I use for calming disturbed animals and assisting recovery of health.

Before you proceed to assist any animal with any healing technique, communicate with them what you would like to do and ensure that they are agreeable to your assistance. I have seen people impose their idea of healing on animals who did not ask for and did not want their "help." To get the best results, the animal needs to be cooperating with you. Willingness is essential to healing. No matter what magical technique or instrument you use, the animal can resist and counteract any physical or mental assistance, if they do not want to get well or be helped by you. Use common sense, humility, and respect in dealing with any being.

The simplest technique is a variation of the ancient art of laying on of hands and is derived from Oriental principles concerning energy flows in the body. Place your hand gently but firmly on different parts of the body, one by one. Slowly lift the hand after holding it a few seconds or longer on each spot, avoiding areas that are too tender for the animal's tolerance.

Injured or ill body parts have stuck energy flows. This technique helps to get the energy moving. The animals will subsequently feel much more in touch with their bodies, thereby increasing circulation and nourishment to the areas touched.

Another method to assist healing is to connect up different body parts with your hands, like an electrical circuit. For example, your horse has a sore spot on her belly. Place one hand on or near her belly and another on the back of her head. Avoid spots that are too sensitive or that make the animal jump and resist your touch. You may feel a pulsing or energy exchange between the two points. Hold the spots until the body feels calmer or there is a synchronized pulse in both points. You may then move one hand to another spot, such as opposite the belly, and do the same. Connect up two other points, and continue until the animal feels more relaxed or happy. Some animals fall into a deep, healing sleep, and some may even get up and walk around after not moving for days!

Here's a very gentle massage technique for unlocking tension along the spine and helping to restore better muscular and organic functioning. Rub with the thumb and finger of one hand, or the fingers of both hands, on each side of the spine from the base of the skull to the tail. Gently or firmly press into the muscles, according to the animal's tolerance. Rub all around the hipbones to help balance the lower back, hip, and leg muscles.

Many animals love massage around the neck, ears, and shoulders. It's a good way to get in touch with your animal friends, and when done all over the body, it is also a good way to check their physical condition. I have known dogs who have had tumors or wounds that weren't noticed under long, thick coats until they were overgrown or infected. Practice massage as a preventive measure.

Sometimes an underlying physical condition can aggravate or even cause a behavior problem. I was called to see a dog named Frodo, whose incessant barking was upsetting the neighbors. His person had recently moved from a house to the present apartment. She had tried calming him down, but he jumped up and barked at the slightest noise. According to the neighbors, his barking was loud, frantic, and frequent while she was gone.

When I walked in, Frodo barked at me until I sat down. His person said he did this with everyone. I talked to him and began touching his body gently, checking for sensitive areas, as I have often done during consultations. When I touched the middle of his back, he whipped his head around and warned me with a slight growl and the thought, "Don't touch me there." His person then mentioned that he doesn't let anyone touch him except on his head and shoulders.

I could see from his actions and from subtle perception of the area that there was an energy blockage in his lower spine. The vertebrae looked bunched up and out of alignment. Another noticeable aspect of Frodo's body was that his rear end and legs appeared underdeveloped and somewhat stiff, as if the muscles had atrophied.

Frodo flashed a picture of a car to me, and I asked his person if a car had hit him. She then remembered that he had fallen out of a moving car about seven years ago and had been lame for awhile, but recovered on his own.

I asked her to recall when he started being touchy and barking so much. Sure enough, it was soon after that accident.

She hadn't thought much about it, since they had lived in a house before, with no neighbors near enough to be bothered by his barking.

Noises or anyone approaching him aggravated the suppressed pain from Frodo's injury. He barked to stop the approach of anything or anyone that might hurt that part of his body. After I counseled him on the accident to relieve the mental stress, he relaxed and visibly felt better.

His body still needed some help, but Frodo remained wary of my touching that sensitive area on his back. I used a technique that is helpful with animals who are hurt or frightened, and who may bite or strike out if you directly contact them. After letting him know what I was going to do—*a very important step before one proceeds*—I stroked the air a few inches above his body, from the top to the base of his spine and in other patterns following the body's natural energy flow. This helped to release some of the blocked energy and to relieve stress in his spine.

Frodo's problem couldn't be resolved in one visit. I returned once a week about three times. I could gradually touch his back without his objecting and thus could gently ease the tension from his muscles so that they worked in a more balanced way, which helped the vertebrae into better alignment.

After one visit, his person remarked how his appetite had increased, and how he ate his food more heartily. I asked her to add a few supplements to his food, like bone meal, dolomite, nutritional yeast, and vitamin E, for calming him and assisting muscle and bone healing.

In a few weeks the change in his body was very noticeable. His lower back and leg muscles had filled out, and he no longer looked front-heavy as before.

The greatest thing was that he calmed down considerably and could pay more attention to the request to bark only when strangers approached the apartment. By my last visit, he had no resistance to being touched firmly anywhere on his body. He was relaxed and much happier, as were his person and neighbors.

The results from any of these simple home procedures can be miraculous, especially if they are combined with natural health care, veterinary treatment, and counseling to locate and clear up the mental or spiritual side of the problem.

In following these procedures, be empathetic but maintain enough emotional distance to be effective. Projecting an overly sympathetic or anxious attitude can prolong illness by increasing the animal's dependence on you. Respect your animal companion's individuality and ability to heal his or her own body, with the right help, and watch for the favorable response.

THE FUTURE OF

LIFE FORMS

ON EARTH

ANIMALS AND CHILDREN

PEOPLE LOSE THEIR childhood ability to communicate with animals partly because of negative adult attitudes and lack of positive exposure to animals. Even with enlightened parents who respect animals as fellow beings, the child's communication ability may be hindered by abuse or lack of use, or from not being properly trained in how to handle and communicate with animals.

In an animal communication training center for children and parents that I envision for the future, young children and animals would be encouraged in their natural tendencies to be interested in and communicate with other life forms. Human and non-human participants would be educated in good communication and handling of each other. It would be a safe environment for all to expand their relationships.

Here are some of the results of providing children with good exposure to animals:

In 1978 a woman named Debbie was studying my techniques of body movement and dance. A few months after her daughter, Samantha, was born, Debbie brought her to the lessons. Pasha, my male Afghan, then about six months old, was always excited to see Samantha, welcoming her with enthusiastic leaps and kisses. Samantha would physically return Pasha's greeting by looking and reaching for him as she was able, and they both enjoyed each other's company.

When my female Afghan, Miel, then about eight weeks old, met Samantha when she was a year old, Samantha was eager to grab Miel. We let her know that Miel was a puppy and needed gentle treatment. It was Miel's first encounter with a child, and I wanted it to be a good one for her. With our guidance, Samantha and Miel had a good introduction.

Joan, another lovely person who studied dance with me, also enjoyed my dogs. Her son Reme (pronounced "ray-me") was five months old when he met Pasha, then about fifteen months old. They really loved each other, though we had to moderate Pasha's abundant expressiveness to match Reme's physical size. One time, when Joan and Reme came for dance class, Reme crawled over to Pasha, who was lying down quietly after his initial exuberant greeting. Reme looked at Pasha, and Pasha looked at Reme, directly and totally communicating as beings, with no consideration about their difference in species. After awhile Reme whapped his hand down on Pasha, and Pasha duplicated his gesture and whapped his paw on Reme. They both loved their mutual game, and it was thrilling to watch them.

Of course, it's necessary to train both child and animal companion in the right amount of contact to use and not let them get hurt in their urges to get to know each other. Once, when Miel was a few months old, she cried as Reme grabbed her too forcefully. We showed Reme how to be gentle with her. Miel was also advised that she did not have to experience undesired physical contact and could withdraw.

You have to allow for individual differences in how much contact an animal or child will want and enjoy, and handle them accordingly. Human babies like to grab and pull and explore everything, and other young animals like to sniff, lick, jump, chew, and play. It can be a fiasco when they first meet, without some supervision. You need to understand and work with each species' behavior patterns and the individual's needs. If you show children how to approach another animal in a way that is acceptable to the animal and vice versa, they'll soon establish their own understanding. The telepathic communication behind it all will continue as the child grows, as long as it's acknowledged and allowed to be expressed.

The results of this early exposure for both Samantha and Reme were amazingly evident at one Thanksgiving celebration we had at our home. Several children were there, including Samantha, then a little over two years, and Reme, about one and one-half. Miel was then over a year old, so the children had two large dogs to handle. When Samantha wanted to eat something as she walked around, she let the dogs know that it was hers, and gently but firmly pushed them aside when she wanted to go by. Reme also talked to and walked among the dogs confidently.

I realized why these children were so able to handle animals when I saw another child, about two and one-half years old. She clung to her mother and was not even able to look at the dogs when they came near, even though they approached with gentle sniffing. It was obvious that she had not had much positive exposure to animals.

With the right exposure and education, I have seen a one-year-old girl walk and play among nine large dogs with minimum supervision needed. You can encourage children's good communication and handling of animals by early, even prenatal, demonstrations of positive attitudes and good experiences. Start with well-treated, trustworthy animals, and expose children gradually, controlling the physical contact calmly.

Don't let children hurt animals in their enthusiasm for contact or put animals in situations where they may bite or claw to get away from unwanted hair pulling or screaming. Child or adult fear of animals or animals' fear of children can be overcome by setting up safe situations to contact and withdraw, in acceptable doses for all concerned.

Talk to both children and animal companions about what you'd like from each regarding the other. Be patient and enlist their cooperation and understanding. They'll get it and respond wonderfully in most cases.

We are cohabitants of this world. A way to understand each other better is by making contact and opportunities to communicate safely available, especially for young ones. I believe there will come a day when all species are reunited in close connection and cooperation, whereby we walk among each other not with fear but with peaceful communion. There will then be no need to have animals live in zoos or animal parks for humans to experience their beauty and have them teach us who they are and who we are together. We will move among each other freely, without artificial barriers. Can you envision this era of harmony among all species?

HUMAN SUPERIORITY COMPLEX

This section may require a daring spiritual leap into unexplored regions. If it all seems too unreal, just pass it by as not true for you at this time, or accept it as my personal experience to stimulate further thought. It may even explain a few things that you hadn't understood about your animal friends previously. Thoughts to ponder:

Some people find it hard to look through the viewpoint of an animal or imagine what it would be like to be a species other than human. They ask me, "Why would anyone want to be a dog, cat, or bird? It's degrading." They assume that human bodies are the ultimate status or the most advanced or intelligent forms, and that it is somehow inferior or substandard to "be" a nonhuman animal.

This generalized idea may stem from the reincarnation theory or philosophies or religions that propose that beings evolve from simple (lower) to more complex (higher) body forms as they spiritually advance, and/or that you can't attain full spiritual completion until you are human. This includes the idea that humans are the top of the line or the chosen ones, and the rest are relatively unaware of their own identity or just unconscious.

I have not found this to be the case in my experience counseling thousands of people and other animals. Beings who have had human bodies may now have animal forms or the reverse, for various reasons and with no general set pattern that applies to all.

Some people also assume, from their narrow perspective of not seeing the interrelationship of all beings, that animals, plants, and minerals contribute little to life. They feel that humans create the best and biggest games or have the most choice and the most fun, so it would be boring or limiting to be anything but human.

This "human superiority complex" prevents full observation and recognition of who animals really are. It inhibits the learning and enrichment that is possible from close association with them.

Before I relate my viewpoints and experience on why beings assume animal forms, I would like to take you on a trip that may enlarge your view of this subject.

Imagine yourself outside the physical universe (even 1000 miles above planet Earth will do), looking down through the world of matter and focusing on the bodies that you and other beings are guiding from place to place on planets such as ours. Notice how little they look—like microscopic specks. Now, tell me, what is the difference between operating human versus nonhuman animal specks? From this expanded viewpoint, what is the big deal about being human?

Now take a reverse journey, and zoom back down onto the Earth, and enter into an ant colony. Observe and listen to their activities and exchange of communications. Notice the complexity of social interaction, the cooperation, and the rivalry. Feel the emotions and variety of thought interplay. Does this remind you of any other species you may be particularly connected with?

For more adventure, go microscopic, and experience the interactions and moods (yes, moods) of microbes. Notice differences and similarities to your human experience.

When you really connect with or get inside the lives of other creatures—animal, plant, or mineral—it is astounding how fascinating life can be from these perspectives. Human life is not the only or ultimate life. It's part of the web of experience. Spirit flows through all of life, and stripped of all disguises, we are of the same essence.

FROM LIFE TO LIFE

Now, from communication and close association with other animals, I'll relate some discoveries about and reasons for taking on different bodily forms from life to life.

1. Familiarity with the game—e.g., has been a horse for centuries, enjoys it, and easily adopts the lifestyle and identity as his or her own.

2. Desire to be close to other beings, such as human friends. Being born as a dog, cat, or horse is an easy way to reunite on a different or possibly more advantageous basis than as a human baby, which may not be possible for the time or situation, anyway.

Some beings who appear as people's dogs, cats, ducks, or birds are guardians or helpmates and want to serve their "masters" in any way they can. They may have lived together before as human friends, brothers, lovers, or spouses, or have been looking after their people from the spiritual realm as guides. I find that the more spiritually aware people attract animal friends who are highly aware and who have often been with them in the past, sometimes as humans.

One cat I met had the specific purpose to see her person attain spiritual advancement. When the person was not doing the study that would help her expand spiritually, the cat would withdraw, refuse to communicate, and act antagonistically until her person got back on track again.

When I lived in the cabin in Los Angeles, Pasha used to knock on my door and lay his paw on my face at the time of the morning I had previously decided to get up, to ensure I stuck to my plans. If I told him to go away, as I wanted to sleep a little longer, he'd come back in ten minutes or so and try again.

Many animals desire to help and even enlighten other beings, and are devoted to their human companion's welfare.

3. Stuck in past traumatic incidents and under compulsion to be that type of body (as many humans are).

A particular aspect of this is when beings who feel they have transgressed against a type of person or animal will make amends by appearing in that type of body in their next life. The wealthy tyrant may become a pauper.

One rabbit I counseled was unhappy being domesticated and in a cage. He had previously lived as a fox who was shot while he killed a domestic rabbit in her cage. He had felt guilty about catching prey who had no chance to get away, and the next thing he knew he was wiggling his nose and looking up at his human caretakers.

I met a jaguar who was miserably pacing and howling in a cage in a zoo. I felt very bad about him, so I sat quietly nearby and asked him why he was there. He sent me pictures of having illegally poached big cats, including jaguars, as a man in his last life. While I still felt compassion for his present suffering, I could understand how he brought this situation to himself. The wheel seems to come around to help us learn all the ways to experience life with understanding and compassion.

4. Wants to have a variety of interesting experiences or just plain fun—flying for a few years as an eagle, leaping lightly as a lizard, or running seventy miles per hour as a cheetah, enjoying the adventures and aesthetics of different life forms.

I had a hamster friend named Tumi, who at about one and one-half years of age (old as hamsters go) developed a cough, which I knew meant her time to depart was coming soon. I asked her if she wanted to have a fling out in the woods instead of dying slowly in her current home. She thought that would be fun. I warned her beforehand of the risks of being caught by predators.

I heard her at night rustling through the leaves and coughing, after she had left the safety of her hutch. So, I went out after her to make sure that she knew she was alerting every predator of her presence and probably would meet a swift death. She understood, and at first came toward me to be carried to safety. At the last minute, she changed her mind and happily dashed back out toward the woods.

The next morning I was aware that she had been killed after a fun few hours in the woods. Upon contacting her, she flashed me a picture of a raccoon, who had eaten her. The raccoon had caught her, and she left her body and watched the proceedings from above. She so admired the beauty of the raccoon, that she then decided that would be her next life experience. She ecstatically went off to become a baby raccoon.

5. Confusion, owing to a precipitous or painful death for which they were not prepared, led them to land in the closest new body available.

6. Desire to observe life from a safe or comfortable viewpoint, otherwise known as taking a break.

I have met dogs who are quite happy with their people's awareness of them as "just" dogs, without many expectations of them. They relax and have time to recover from or work out their last life experience. Some beings do this in the spiritual realm between lives, while others find it better to do the sorting-out process in their next incarnation, yet out of the fray.

I met a horse who did not want to do any of the activities that humans expected of him. He had thought, when he saw horses from his past human viewpoint, that they had an easy life of grazing and meditating. As a horse, that's all he wanted to do. Surprise! He still had to work things out with humans, though he had wanted to get away from that.

7. Unawareness or desire to hide. Many beings have little or no conscious choice about the lives they lead. They haven't a clue as to why they're here, who they are, or what they're doing. Does this sound familiar?

I find this more common in Western, industrialized, human society than among other animals, but you find all degrees of spiritual awareness among different life forms.

There are many individual variations for taking any type of animal or human body or that particular animal body. I could tell a million tails—oops, tales!

HARMONY AND UNITY

When you observe and relate to animals, you find much to admire and learn from them. Some of the most loved traits of many companion animals are their desires to serve and fulfill a purpose, assist humankind with devotion and loyalty, give love and be loved, accept you as you are, entertain with their play and love for life, and make you happy.

I consider it a privilege to associate with many fine, wise, and wonderful animal individuals. That many choose, with their powerful forms (horses, elephants, whales, to name a few), to cooperate with humans is at times amazing, especially considering the abuse many humans heap upon them. Their ability to forgive and keep trying to teach and help is sometimes beyond human comprehension. Wild animals can also be appreciated for their beauty, the fascinating experience of understanding their life patterns and viewpoints, their role in the balance and unity of all life on Earth, and the completeness and fulfillment we feel in association with them.

In general, I have not found nonhuman animals to be some lower form of being. In fact, I meet many animals who are far more intelligent, perceptive, purposeful, and able to enjoy life to the fullest than many humans are. Besides, it's fun to experience different bodies and use the experience of, say, leaping as a frog in order to enhance your gymnastic ability, or being agile and fierce as a tiger to better master the human game! We all help to complete each other.

Animals are individuals with their own unique histories, and we all can learn an immense amount from communicating with and "being" them. The more we comprehend and enjoy the vastness of experience of the many forms in this universe, the more we participate in the infinity of creation that expresses spirit in its fullness.

Here's to more understanding, enlightenment, harmony and infinite fun together! We are all *anima*.

ABOUT THE AUTHOR

PENELOPE SMITH is a pioneer in the practice of interspecies telepathic communication and has become the world's foremost teacher of basic and advanced courses in this field. In this capacity, she has helped launch the careers of numerous professional animal communicators.

Having communicated with animals telepathically throughout her life, Penelope discovered in 1971 that animals could be relieved of emotional traumas and other problems through the same counseling techniques that benefit humans. Contributing to her success are her degrees in the social sciences; years of training and experience in human counseling, nutrition, and holistic energy balancing methods; research into animal nutrition, anatomy, behavior, and care; and the firsthand education gathered from the thousands of animals she has contacted. She has composed books, audio- and videotapes, and magazine articles. She also publishes a quarterly journal, *Species Link*, and is internationally known as a lecturer and workshop leader.

Penelope feels that the sacred connection we make with other species through telepathic communication is essential for human wholeness. She believes that everyone is born with the power to communicate with other species; although most people have put aside and forgotten this gift, it can be reclaimed for the benefit of all beings on Earth. She lives with her animal family in the woods of Inverness Ridge, adjacent to Point Reyes National Seashore, northwest of San Francisco.

AUDIOTAPES

ANIMAL DEATH

A Spiritual Journey

ISBN 0-936552-09-3; 90 minutes; $14.95

The death of an animal companion is often a painful and confusing experience for those left behind. The subject of animal death from a spiritual perspective is explored by this audiotape. Both informative and comforting, it fathoms the process of dying (from animals' and people's viewpoints), working through guilt and grieving, recognizing when to consider euthanasia, understanding what happens after animals depart from the physical body, and coming to terms with reincarnation—meeting your friends from life to life. The recording includes a guided visualization to help you communicate with a departed animal friend.

THE INTERSPECIES TELEPATHIC CONNECTION TAPE SERIES

This series of six digitally recorded audio-cassettes on four major topics covers the theory and practice of direct communication, mind-to-mind and heart-to-heart, with other species. The cassettes offer guidance in breaking through the layers of cultural conditioning that inhibit clear reception of communication from animals, solving problems and understanding an animal companion's behavior, and realizing deeper levels of mutual understanding and cooperation. Filled with timeless wisdom, these cassettes can be played again and again to further personal growth.

Tapes 1–4 below conveniently packaged in an aesthetically delightful album. ISBN 0-936552-12-3; 6 hours; $59.95

1. HOW TO COMMUNICATE WITH ANIMALS: THE STEPS
A do-it-yourself mini-workshop for those eager to become more attuned to animals.
ISBN 0-936552-13-1; 1 hour

2. ANIMAL INTELLIGENCE AND AWARENESS
How intelligent are animals? Is *Homo sapiens* the only species that is self-aware? Learn how other animals' comprehension, rea-

soning, and awareness compare to human ability, based on actual telepathic communication and observable responses from animals. This casssette is guaranteed to jog your preconceptions and stimulate your intelligence and awareness.

ISBN 0-936552-14-X; 1 hour

3. Understanding Animals' Viewpoints

Get the "inside story" on how animals view humans and the world around them. Numerous experiences reveal animals' purposes, sense of humor, deep feelings, and spiritual insights. This cassette helps to release preconceived notions that can block your communication and connection with other species, and opens you to seeing through your animal companion's eyes.

ISBN 0-936552-15-8; 2 hours

4. Healing and Counseling with Animals

Learn straightforward methods to help animals work through emotional trauma, fear, injury, illness, and death. While not a substitute for veterinary assistance, this cassette promotes the understanding of physical and spiritual healing: bodywork and counseling, both in-person and at a distance; contacting animals who have died; spirit transfer; entities. The listener gains insights into Penelope's seasoned approach to communicating with and counseling animals.

ISBN 0-936552-16-8; 2 hours

VIDEOTAPE

Telepathic Communication with Animals

This videotape is an introduction and overview of the subject—an eye-opener for skeptics! Penelope Smith demonstrates ways of increasing our understanding of and harmony with other species. She also clarifies the fundamental importance of heightening our awareness of other animals' spiritual nature and expanding our abilities to fully communicate with them.

We witness consultations and interviews with people who, together with their animal companions, have benefited from Penelope's communication, counseling, and healing work. In scenes of workshops, we view a sampling of techniques that help people regain their power to telepathically communicate with other species.

ISBN 0-916289-11-7; VHS, 46 minutes; $29.95

Produced by Kelly Hart/Hartworks (non-VHS formats available)

PERIODICAL

Species Link

The Journal of Interspecies Telepathic Communication

If you love animals and are open to the possibility of communicating with other species, if you desire to learn as much as you can about telepathic communication with animals, or if you are already a practitioner in this field, *Species Link* is vital for you! In issues of this fascinating journal, read factual accounts of beneficial telepathic communications with animals, as well as contributions of prose and poetry transcribed directly from communications with our nonhuman friends.

You will find tested methods for learning and teaching inter-species telepathic communication, books and other resources that help to increase understanding of other life forms, a current directory of animal communication practitioners, plus readers' stories, poems, art, book reviews, and letters.

Species Link is a forum and network for sharing experiences, helpful hints, insights, humor, growth along the path, and the joy of deep understanding and heightened awareness of all beings. The journal's motto: Brotherhood/Sisterhood ... Inspiration ... Transformation.

$20 per year; single issues $6

Please write or call for information on Penelope Smith's lectures and workshops.

Pegasus Publications
P.O. Box 1060
    Point Reyes Station, CA 94956-1060
Phone: (415) 663-1247
Fax: (415) 663-8260

OTHER BOOKS FROM BEYOND WORDS PUBLISHING, INC.

ADULTS

WHEN ANIMALS SPEAK

Lessons, Healings, and Teachings for Humanity

Author: Penelope Smith; Foreword: Michael Roads

$14.95, softcover

This book offers deep, life-changing revelations, communicated directly from the animals. Discover who animals and other forms of life really are; how they understand themselves and others; how they feel about humans and life on Earth; how they choose their paths in life and death; the depth of their spiritual understanding and purposes; and how they can teach, heal, and guide us back to wholeness as physical, mental, emotional, and spiritual beings. Regain the language natively understood by all species. Laugh as you experience other species' refreshing and sometimes startling points of view on living in this world, among humans, and with you.

Dolphin Talk

An Animal Communicator Shares Her Connection

Author: Penelope Smith

$9.95, audiotape

Tales of adventure and communications from the dolphins transport us into the excitement and mystery of our eternal connection with these charismatic marine mammals. Smith shares the dolphin healing journey that enabled her to overcome a lifelong fear of deep water and swim with wild dolphins in the open ocean. Feel the special affection for the human species that the dolphins impart; hear about the merging of dolphin and human consciousness; experience the haunting tones of dolphin "resounding skull bone chanting," creating an opening in the listener's skull to better receive the dolphin's energetic transformations. According to Smith, the dolphins facilitate the weaving of energy matrices of consciousness over our planet, allowing receptive and ready humans to receive the dolphins' pure love throughout their cellular structure and to experience telepathic communication. Feel the dolphins' healing power conveyed through this audiotape, directly by them!

KINSHIP WITH THE ANIMALS

Authors: Michael Tobias and Kate Solisti-Mattelon
$15.95, softcover

Contributors to *Kinship with the Animals* represent a myriad of countries and traditions. From Jane Goodall illustrating the emergence of her lifelong devotion to animals, to Linda Tellington-Jones describing her experiences communicating with animals through touch, the thirty-three stories in *Kinship with the Animals* deconstruct traditional notions of animals by offering a new and insightful vision of animals as conscious beings capable of deep feelings and sophisticated thoughts. The editors have deliberately sought stories that present diverse views of animal awareness and communication.

The Holistic Animal Handbook

A Guidebook to Nutrition, Health, and Communication
Authors: Kate Solisti-Mattelon and Patrice Mattelon
$14.95, softcover

The *Holistic Animal Handbook* is the first book to bring together practical information about diet, nutrition, and training with animal communication and emotional balancing techniques. The book is the result of the authors' many years of experience working with companion animals and their people. It includes chapters that explain how to prepare healthy, holistic recipes and Bach Flower Remedies for restoring an animal's emotional balance. There is also a chapter that describes natural techniques for dealing with common behavioral and training problems. The goal of *The Holistic Animal Handbook* is to provide animal guardians with a starting point from which they can foster and practice deeper interspecies communication. Focusing primarily on dogs, cats, and horses but relevant to virtually all animals, the book presents a dual premise: healthy companion animals are better equipped to help the humans they love, just as educated humans are better able to comprehend what their animals are about.

Conversations with Dog

An Uncommon Dogalog of Canine Wisdom
Author: Kate Solisti-Mattelon
$13.95, softcover

Conversations with Dog is a groundbreaking book in the field of human-animal communication. In a question-and-answer format, this is the first book of its kind to pose questions to dogs and receive answers in return. These answers are not based on what human beings suppose dogs think. Instead, Solisti-Mattelon, a practicing animal communicator, goes straight to the dogs themselves. Most of us who own dogs know they are trying to tell us something, and *Conversations with Dog* breaks through the species barrier to ask dogs what they want to tell all of us.

Conversations with Cat

An Uncommon Catalog of Feline Wisdom

Author: Kate Solisti-Mattelon

$13.95, softcover

After disclosing the innermost thoughts of our canine friends in the highly successful *Conversations with Dog*, professional animal communicator Kate Solisti-Mattelon returns to tell the cats' side of the story. Their responses to some of life most challenging questions offer surprising insights into the spiritual, physical, and mental awareness of our feline friends.

Listening to Wild Dolphins

Learning Their Secrets for Living with Joy

Author: Bobbie Sandoz

$14.95, softcover

Listening to Wild Dolphins, written by a well-established therapist, chronicles her remarkable and healing experiences while swimming with a pod of wild dolphins off the shores of her Hawaiian home over the past ten years. She has observed that the dolphins have qualities which humans can model to become more balanced and joyful in everyday life.

The Great Wing

A Parable

Author: Louis A. Tartaglia, M.D.; Foreword: Father Angelo Scolozzi

$14.95, hardcover

The Great Wing transforms the timeless miracle of the migration of a flock of geese into a parable for the modern age. It recounts a young goose's own reluctant but steady transformation from gangly fledgling to Grand Goose and his triumph over the turmoils of his soul and the buffeting of a mighty Atlantic storm. In *The Great Wing*, our potential as individuals is affirmed, as is the power of group prayer, or the "Flock Mind." As we make the journey with this goose and his flock, we rediscover that we tie our own potential into the power of the common good by way of attributes such as honesty, hope, courage, trust, perseverance, spirituality, and service. The young goose's trials and tribulations, as well as his triumph, are our own.

Flower Essences for Animals

Remedies for Helping the Pets You Love
Author: Lila Devi; Foreword: Rena Ferreira, D.V.M.
$14.95, softcover

Flower essences—herbal tinctures for strength and balance—are widely used to treat human ailments and are also a simple and effective means of pet care in both daily life and emergencies. Completely safe and gentle, yet powerful, these essences activate the animals' own ability to heal itself. A brand-new concept of "theme essences" to determine your pet's innate character strengths and your own as a pet owner is included.

For Children

Psychic Pets

Supernatural True Stories of Paranormal Animals
Author: John Sutton
$7.95, softcover

Psychic Pets relates incredible true stories of psychic powers demonstrated by people's animal companions: cats, dogs, and horses that can read minds, foresee the future, transport themselves from one place to another by nonphysical means, see ghosts, and even return as ghosts themselves. You'll be amazed, astounded, and intrigued by what you read. These are recent stories from all over the world, collected by the author through interviews with the human companions.

This book also offers a way to learn if your pet is psychic, through specially designed tests of psychic abilities. In case you discover that your pet is not psychic, the book also provides simple training exercises for developing your pet's psychic powers!

To order or to request a catalog, contact:

Beyond Words Publishing, Inc.
20827 NW Cornell Road, Suite 500
Hillsboro, OR 97124-9808
503-531-8700

You can also visit our Web site at www.beyondword.com
or email us at info@beyondword.com

Beyond Words Publishing, Inc.

Our corporate mission:

Inspire to Integrity

Our declared values:

We give to all of life as life has given to us.

We honor all relationships.

Trust and stewardship are integral to fulfilling dreams.

Collaboration is essential to create miracles.

Creativity and aesthetics nourish the soul.

Unlimited thinking is fundamental.

Living your passion is vital.

Joy and humor open our hearts to growth.

It is important to remind ourselves of love.